MOUNT
UP ON
WOUNDED
WINGS

OVERCOMING
HURTFUL BACKGROUNDS

BENETH PETERS JONES

BJU PRESS
GREENVILLE, SOUTH CAROLINA

Library of Congress Cataloging-in-Publication Data

Jones, Beneth Peters, date.
    Mount up on wounded wings / Beneth Peters Jones.
        p.   cm.
    ISBN 0-89084-772-X
    1. Abused Women—Pastoral counseling of. 2. Christian women—
    Religious life. I. Title.
    BV4445.5.J66 1994
    248.8' 6' 082—dc20   94-28759
                                                                    CIP

NOTE:
The fact that materials produced by other publishers are referred to in this volume
does not constitute an endorsement by BJU Press of the content or theological
position of materials produced by such publishers. The position of BJU Press, and
of Bob Jones University itself, is well known. Any references and ancillary materials are listed as an aid to the reader and in an attempt to maintain the accepted
academic standards of the publishing industry.

Mount Up on Wounded Wings

Cover design by Jamie Miller
Edited by Carolyn Cooper and Rebecca Moore

© 1994 BJU Press
Greenville, South Carolina 29614

ISBN 0-89084-772-X

15   14   13   12   11   10   9   8   7   6   5   4   3

DEDICATION
For my dear sisters, Dacia and Pat

Table of Contents

PREFACE

"I'd *like* to write a novel, Lord. I've researched the period, completed several chapters. . . ." But God's quiet, firm impression comes, "Not now. There is something else I'd have you write."

So it is under compulsion from the Lord Jesus, our wounded Savior, and with empathetic love for Christian women wounded in childhood, that I undertake this writing. God alone knows the personal cost in renewed tears, relived agonies, and reopened wounds. If that sacrifice can result in helping just one precious Christian sister, the price is small.

The core concentration is upon God's Word: It is the only effective balm for the kinds of hurts discussed. The text is physically arranged to encourage the reader toward fresh awareness and personal application. Too, it is set in enlarged print for the sake of those who will read through tears. The subject treatment is intentionally short and to the point. Many pages of real-life examples could be given; my heart's focus, however, is upon *you*—the Christian woman of whatever age who is struggling right now because of wounded wings.

The book is intended only to be a branch—a small branch held close to the ground of our mutual experience. It is held with the prayer that you or someone you know might use it as a launching point from which to *Mount Up on Wounded Wings*.

In Him and for Him,
Beneth Peters Jones

Long ago, poet George Herbert drew a beautiful picture of spiritual flight on sin-weakened wings. Although this poem does not refer specifically to *wounded* wings, the thought is nevertheless appropriate. The word *imp* in the next to the last line is a term from falconry referring to the grafting of new feathers onto a bird's wing to repair damage or to increase flying capacity.

Easter Wings

Lord, who createdst man in wealth and store,
Though foolishly he lost the same,
Decaying more and more
Till he became
Most poor:
With thee
O let me rise
As larks, harmoniously,
And sing this day thy victories:
Then shall the fall further the flight in me.

My tender age in sorrow did begin:
And still with sicknesses and shame
Thou didst so punish sin,
That I became
Most thin.
With thee
Let me combine,
And feel this day thy victory;
For, if I imp my wing on thine,
Affliction shall advance the flight in me.

George Herbert
(1593-1633)

CHAPTER ONE
FOUL OR FOWL?

This book is intended for the Christian woman whose home background, like my own, was marred by pain. However, that intention can be frustrated by the reader's capacity to respond. It is imperative, therefore, to lay a solid foundation for my communicating and your using the principles which will be presented. That foundation is absolutely unique.

> *For other foundation can no man lay than that is laid, which is Jesus Christ.*
> *I Corinthians 3:11*

For what is this foundation? It is for spiritual creation and life. The principles of *physical* flight can be applied only by creatures capable of flight. No one with intelligence would expect a fox, a horse, a goat, or a mouse to fly—regardless of its lineage, beauty, or intelligence. But a bird, whether sparrow or eagle, takes naturally to the air. So, too, the principles of *spiritual* flight can be applied only by those whose creation and capability make the principles practicable.

The words *foul* and *fowl* sound exactly alike when pronounced. But how wholly unlike is the reality! Who or what, then, is this flight-intended spiritual creature, the "Christian" woman? What are the marks of identification? Consider the following:

Christian. The term has been so abused and distorted in modern society that its true meaning must be clarified. The Bible urges, "Examine yourselves, whether ye be in the faith" (II Cor. 13:5). Please read this first chapter carefully, prayerfully contemplating your real spiritual condition *in the light of God's Word.*

Christian is frequently used simply to distinguish one portion of population from another, indicating those favoring Christian beliefs and values rather than pagan or Moslem or some other. But *preference* for things Christian over those of atheism, Hinduism, Islam, and others is no more than a mental nod of assent. It leaves such a one a stranger to the Person of the Lord Jesus Christ, who said,

> *I am the way, the truth, and the life: no*
> *man cometh unto the Father, but by me.*
> *John 14:6*

Further, the title *Christian* is claimed by some on the basis of national, church, or family affiliation.

But one's *temporal* location has no connection with one's *eternal* safety and destination. The Lord Jesus Christ, God become man, pronounced the following:

> *My kingdom is not of this world.*
> *John 18:36*

*Verily, verily, I say unto thee, Except a man
be born again, he cannot see the kingdom
of God.*

John 3:3

Still more specifically, *Christian* may be taken to designate individuals who have "always believed in God" or whose youthful confirmation, baptism, or conversion has been faithfully and frequently related by family members.

But having been subjected to or assured by some human or institutional word, one is led into a comfortable state of mind that may blind one to the actual state of her soul.

*That which is born of the flesh is flesh;
and that which is born of the Spirit is spirit.*

John 3:6

*Flesh and blood cannot inherit the king-
dom of God; neither doth corruption inherit
incorruption.*

I Corinthians 15:50

Finally, *Christian* too often is a long-held, feeling-based or form-originated tag—a designation strengthened through many years by multiple raisings of the hand or other responses to pulpit appeals.

But feelings and form have nothing to do with eternal reality.

*For in Christ Jesus neither circumcision
availeth any thing, nor uncircumcision, but
a new creature.*

Galatians 6:15

*Not every one that saith unto me, Lord,
Lord, shall enter into the kingdom of
heaven; but he that doeth the will of my*

*Father which is in heaven. Many will say
to me in that day, Lord, Lord, have we not
prophesied in thy name? and in thy name
have cast out devils? and in thy name done
many wonderful works? And then will I
profess unto them, I never knew you: depart
from me, ye that work iniquity.*

Matthew 7:21-23

God, who is a spirit, is perfect in His holiness and perfect in His justice. As such, He demands that the eternal part of these human selves, our spirits (or souls), be made *fit to dwell with Him forever.* Each of us must become *a new creature.* Why is this transformation necessary? Because the old creature—humanity in its unredeemed state—is *fouled* by sin.

The Bible draws a clear picture of the human soul's dilemma. We are sinful by nature, and we are also sinful *in practice.* Sin is imperfection, which offends God's holiness. In His absolute purity God must stand apart from sin's foulness.

*Your iniquities have separated between you
and your God.*

Isaiah 59:2

Think of that separation as an immense chasm. Far down in its depths lies hell, the unspeakably awful place where Satan, his demons, and unredeemed sinners will spend eternity, condemned by God's perfect justice. There is no way for feeble humanity to build a bridge strong enough or long enough to span the chasm. Pride leads us to attempt such a bridge using match sticks of intellect, logs of good deeds, timbers of church membership, or steel girders of self-sacrifice. All are futile.

> *For as many as are of the works of the law*
> *are under the curse: for it is written, Cursed*
> *is every one that continueth not in all*
> *things which are written in the book of the*
> *law to do them. But that no man is justi-*
> *fied by the law in the sight of God, it is evi-*
> *dent: for, The just shall live by faith.*
> Galatians 3:10-11

There is, then, only one solution: it springs from the loving heart of God, who is

> *. . . not willing that any should perish, but*
> *that all should come to repentance.*
> II Peter 3:9

Wonderfully motivated by His heart of love is His hand of limitless power. Yearning to have us know and dwell with Him, God *bridges* the chasm—bridges it with the cross of Calvary.

> *For God so loved the world, that he gave*
> *his only begotten Son, that whosoever be-*
> *lieveth in him should not perish, but have*
> *everlasting life.*
> John 3:16

Think further about the matter. In order to be fit for God's presence and thereby genuinely able to bear the name *Christian* (literally, a Christ-follower), an individual must *personally* appropriate the cross of Calvary as her passage to spiritual safety. That involves four things.

1. *Recognition of personal sinfulness.* Sin is fall-ing short of God's standard: perfection. Compared to other members of the human race, we may seem "good." God nevertheless sees us as sinful—unfit to be in His presence. His standard for humanity is contained in the

Ten Commandments. Righteousness demands conformity to those commandments—each and all of them.

> *For whosoever shall keep the whole law, and*
> *yet offend in one point, he is guilty of all.*
>
> *James 2:10*

Having defined sin as the breaking of His commandments, God proclaims the plight which faces each of us individually.

> *The soul that sinneth, it shall die. The son*
> *shall not bear the iniquity of the father, nei-*
> *ther shall the father bear the iniquity of the*
> *son: the righteousness of the righteous shall*
> *be upon him, and the wickedness of the*
> *wicked shall be upon him.*
>
> *Ezekiel 18:20*

> *For the wages of sin is death.*
>
> *Romans 6:23*

The death spoken of is eternal separation from God, who is Life.

2. *Recognition of personal helplessness.* We could strive mightily night and day, live sacrificially toward our fellow man, flagellate our bodies in order to render ourselves worthy, and so forth; but *nothing* we can do or say impresses a thrice-holy God.

> *The sacrifice of the wicked is an abomina-*
> *tion to the Lord.*
>
> *Proverbs 15:8*

> *The plowing of the wicked is sin.*
>
> *Proverbs 21:4*

*So then they that are in the flesh cannot
please God.*

Romans 8:8

*But we are all as an unclean thing, and all
our righteousnesses are as filthy rags; and
we all do fade as a leaf; and our iniquities,
like the wind, have taken us away.*

Isaiah 64:6

**3. Personal acknowledgment that God alone
can rescue from sin and recognition that He has
provided salvation through Jesus Christ, His Son.**
The same verse which knells the mandatory death sentence for sin, "the wages of sin is death," goes on to
proclaim release from that judgment.

*But the gift of God is eternal life through
Jesus Christ our Lord.*

Romans 6:23

**4. Personal repentance of sin and acceptance of
salvation in the person of Jesus Christ.** Salvation
means *rescue*—rescue from the foulness of sin. It means
freedom from sin's power.

*If the Son therefore shall make you free, ye
shall be free indeed.*

John 8:36

The precious shed blood of Jesus Christ not only
cleanses; it *re-creates.*

*Therefore if any man be in Christ, he is a
new creature: old things are passed away;
behold, all things are become new.*

II Corinthians 5:17

That new creature no more is besmirched and bound by sin's foulness.

> *For sin shall not have dominion over you:*
> *for ye are not under the law, but under*
> *grace.*
>
> *Romans 6:14*

While salvation—the new birth—takes place in an instant, sanctification—the new *bearing*—is to be evident throughout all the remainder of one's earthly life. After all, how is any creature properly identified by onlookers? How is it distinguished from others? *By appearance and action.*

Were it possible for a frog to be instantly transformed into a bird, everything about the new creature would be evidently different: its appearance, its choice of environment, and its behavior.

So too it is with the Christian. Having made the crossing to eternal safety, her daily life should demonstrate that she is a new creature—that her heart beats in love for Him who loved her. Jesus explained to His disciples,

> *He that hath my commandments, and*
> *keepeth them, he it is that loveth me.*
>
> *John 14:21*

New minds seek daily cleansing from earth's dust through God's Word.

> *Now ye are clean through the word which I*
> *have spoken unto you.*
>
> *John 15:3*

Those who are the *foul* made *fowl* are marked by the shunning of sin and the seeking of sanctification. There is a blessed "double seal" marking the true believer.

> *Nevertheless the foundation of God stan-*
> *deth sure, having this seal, The Lord*
> *knoweth them that are his. And, Let every*
> *one that nameth the name of Christ depart*
> *from iniquity.*
>
> *II Timothy 2:19*

Do *you* bear that double seal? Does God know you as being truly His—re-created, obedient, and beloved? Does His Spirit speak softly to your heart?

> *O my dove, thou art in the clefts of the*
> *rock, in the secret places of the stairs, let*
> *me see thy countenance, let me hear thy*
> *voice; for sweet is thy voice, and thy counte-*
> *nance is comely.*
>
> *Song of Solomon 2:14*

And do you consistently strive against iniquity, seeking by the enabling of the Holy Spirit and the instruction of the Word to grow more like Christ?

But you may ask, "Why all this concentration on *my* spiritual condition? Why think about *my* sinfulness—I've been *sinned against!*" The answer is simple. A frog, a fish, or a cat can never fly; a *bird* can. A woman who is alive only in the flesh cannot use scriptural principles which apply to the spirit. God promises only to His beloved ones the ability to "mount up with wings as eagles" (Isa. 40:31).

If, after carefully studying the points just presented, you have a settled assurance that you have met the criteria God establishes in Scripture, read on. You are, according to God's Word, a new creature. In the terminology which will be used throughout this book, you are not *foul* but *fowl*, having access to the same limitless power to *heal your hurts* as you had to *save your soul*.

CHAPTER TWO
THE WOUNDING

In beginning a discussion of home wounds, I want to make clear what is *not* meant. We live in a day when both unsaved and saved people shun personal responsibility. Rather than recognize self-fault and failure, the current response to pressure is a cop-out: pointing at something or someone else and saying, in effect, *"That's* the cause of my problem; I'm not to blame. I can't help being the way I am or doing what I do!" *God does not accept blame-shifting.*

> *For we must all appear before the judgment seat of Christ; that every one may receive the things done in his body, according to that he hath done, whether it be good or bad.*
> *II Corinthians 5:10*

This book is not intended to help you create even a single excuse for yourself. *No one* comes from a perfect home, because such a home nowhere exists. Every family will, inevitably, fail in some measure to meet the needs of its members. That truth simply reflects our fallen human state. To pout over, whine about, and accuse parental shortcomings you have magnified is not only shameful but also clearly contrary to the theme of personal accountability which runs through the Bible.

The wounding home is one which grossly distorts God's intended purpose. The popular catch phrase of the moment is *dysfunctional home*. Neat. Clinical. And utterly devoid of reality's agony.

Home. Surely that is one of the most beautiful words in any language. Home should be all the warm, happy, fuzzy things of childhood bliss; it should contain, above all other places, joy, acceptance, encouragement, and nurturing. But the "shoulds" of this world are seldom realized. The missed mark, and its consequences, are nowhere more apparent than in the hurtful home.

In principle, each of us knows the centrality of home, its crucial importance. The frequency and nature of its *harms* have only recently been allowed into the light after years of being suspected or spoken of in whispers. The cloak of secrecy has been particularly thick in the Christian community: we have wanted to believe that the uglies of harmful homes were restricted to the unsaved world—where they "belong." That unintentional smugness must end.

The Need for Exposure

A forthright discussion of child-wounding homes is pertinent and timely for today's Christian woman in the following ways:

The girl or woman coming from a happy home, while more deeply appreciating her own blessings, also needs to develop informed concern for hurting women around her. She must, first, be awakened to the realities so that she does not exacerbate wounds through carelessness or ignorance. Second, she needs to be shaken from complacency and moved to a compelling compassion.

After a seminar session dealing with shattered home backgrounds, a middle-aged lady approached me in tears. She told me, brokenly, that God had used the discussion to open her eyes to her daughter-in-law's problems; suddenly she could understand the reasons for attitudes and actions in the young woman. Understanding had swept away her own impatience and put in its place deep concern and the desire to help.

Impossible as it may seem, statistics bear out the fact that *each* reader of this book has within her circle of acquaintances at least one who comes from a wounding home background. Whoever and wherever she is, that person needs someone to whom she can reach out for understanding and compassion.

Women in full-time Christian ministry and thus serving as counselors need to be familiar with the information that follows. In fact, the question "How can I help women who carry deep hurts from their childhood?" coming from pastors' wives across the country was one of the things God used to break down my resistance to writing this book.

The girl or woman who has personally experienced an unhappy home can directly benefit from the material. First, that one whose wound has been healed can, by briefly retracing her own recovery, come to fuller rejoicing over God's demonstrated power in her life as well as to a strengthened resolve to make herself available to help others. Second, that hurt one whose wound remains raw and inflamed can at last not only know there is hope for healing, but also find the prescription for the Great Physician's balm. The pages which follow, for that latter person, will be difficult; the book's contents may be manageable only in small doses because of the ugly, cutting memories which will rise. That very renewal of pain, however, can be helpful—not only by encouraging a realistic examination of something perhaps never fully faced in oneself but also by creating an awareness that agonies such as those locked within her are neither unique nor rare. In fact, they are as old as humanity. The psalmist expressed internal pain long ago.

> *For I am poor and needy, and my heart is*
> *wounded within me.*
>
> *Psalm 109:22*

Most important, that hurting one can be helped to realize that *wings wounded in childhood do not mean lifelong crippling.*

The Bible tells us that while the prophet Jeremiah "was yet shut up in the court of the prison," God presented him with a challenge and a promise. The same applies to each one who today feels imprisoned by her past.

> *Call unto me, and I will answer thee, and*
> *shew thee great and mighty things, which*
> *thou knowest not.*
>
> *Jeremiah 33:3*

Life's Cruelties

Contrary to fairy tales and wishes, real life has sharp edges. We more or less expect those edges to make themselves felt when we are adults. By that time a person at least has some ability to cope. The most monstrous life wounds are those received in childhood—when physically, mentally, and emotionally the victim is cruelly taken advantage of, when he or she is helpless.

One spring day my daughter and my niece went with me to visit a nearby farm. As we entered the driveway, we noticed on our right a tiny, still-wet calf wobbling about on knobby legs, bawling pitifully. Though cows all around were grazing or suckling their own young, this little fellow was woefully alone, his frantic cries unanswered. We stopped the car, walked to the fence, and watched to see what was happening. Nearby was a cow obviously newly relieved of her belly's burden; she was licking a newborn dry. Investigation and logic brought us to the conclusion that what we were seeing was a mother which had borne twin calves—but rejected one. Sure enough, the lonesome newborn finally managed to stagger close to the cow and other calf, begging for attention and milk. The cow, however, did not just refuse the baby's advances; she became enraged and drove it away. We three helpless human females wanted to clobber that dumb cow! Pitiful as it was, that situation was understandable, forgivable—those were dumb animals, incapable of either reason or genuine affection. Such situations among humans are incomprehensible and inexcusable.

Each human being is wonderfully individualistic; uniqueness is built into his every aspect. The home is meant to be the place where that incipient marvel is molded and enriched, prepared for success and accomplishment. When a home instead attacks its young, it commits treachery. The magnitude of such treachery is expressed by the psalmist.

> *Yea, mine own familiar friend, in whom I*
> *trusted, which did eat of my bread, hath*
> *lifted up his heel against me.*
>
> *Psalm 41:9*

What more "familiar friend" should one have than the members of her own blood family? In whom should one be more able to put entire trust than in those who daily eat with her at the home table? Yet in the wounding home, it is *they* who lift up the heel to kick and crush.

Look again at the Scripture verse just quoted. The *spirit* of the writer is both interesting and instructive. The psalmist here is speaking of his great wounding by trusted friends. Moreover, earlier verses indicate that the treachery came at a time of special vulnerability—when the psalmist was physically ill. However, the statement is direct, simple, and factual. There is neither pitiful breast-beating nor smoldering anger. Rather, a spirit of sadness comes through from his wounded heart. May that be true of you and me as we go on to consider various types of wounding homes. May we leave them in the realm of fact, not allowing tides of anger and hostility to sweep in upon us. Sadness will come, no doubt; but not a one-dimensional sorrow for ourselves alone. Even at this early point in the discussion, recognize that our *hurters* are to be pitied as well. Some wounded in ignorance, unintentionally. Some inflicted wounds out of their own pain. Some had minds twisted by sin's products or practice. Some may even today weep bitter tears of regret in the dark silence of missed blessings and shattered relationships.

Types of Hurtful Home Backgrounds

My own and other women's tears over our childhood's long shadows indicate that homes can wound in many different ways. No particular order or degree of hurt is intended by the sequence in which they will be discussed. Also, be aware that a defective home may exemplify more than one of these types, even several.

The inconsistent Christian home. Tragically common, though seldom recognized for its hurtfulness, this home operates under a veneer of spirituality. But behind closed doors there is denial of everything claimed: standards kept with the lips are broken by the lives. The tone of such a home may be "Do as I say, not as I do"; or it may take a slightly different form: "What you're hearing in church and school is okay to a point. But here in real life things have to be different. . . ." The child growing up in such a sham home is confused and hurt by the contradictions.

The neglectful home. In such a home, father and mother can be characterized by a shrug. They do not show open hostility toward the child; they just do not seem to care about her. The little one is left to grow up untended, like a weed in an overgrown garden. For all practical purposes she is not there; the parents' lives focus past or through her.

The rejecting home. Parents in this type of home express their negative attitudes more strongly; they shove their child aside, as it were, making it plain that she is a nuisance, unwanted. In some cases, the rejection is carried on in silence; parental coldness freezes the youngster's heart. In other instances, the rejection is verbal. But whether silent, spoken quietly, or shouted, the message is clear: "You're a burden; why were you ever born?"

Rejection may be subtle; it may take the form of dissatisfaction. The child is made to feel flawed, never able to please her parents, forever falling short of their expectations or demands.

Rejection may also be comparative: one child is made to feel ugly, stupid, or incompetent by verbal or insinuated contrasts or comparisons. I remember, for instance, a college girl who confided to me that her mother had always compared her unfavorably with her sister, charging her with ugliness and stupidity while extolling her sister's beautiful brilliance. The poor girl had accepted her mother's negative valuation; she was convinced that she was hopelessly deficient.

Finally, rejection may be cloaked in "comic" vestments. Parents may unwittingly or maliciously wound a child with subtle, sharp twigs of ridicule. Sometimes it takes the form of negative nicknames: Skinny Goat, Lumpy Louie, Stumblebum.

The unsaved home. In this home there is disgust, dislike, or scorn toward the born-again child; pressure is put upon her to "loosen up" and "get real." There may be deliberate humiliation as the family and their friends gang up against the Christian, ridiculing her beliefs and behavior. Such a home may be said to wear a sneer—an ugly parental expression which remains burned into the offspring's memory.

The alcoholic/drug-abusing home. In this household there are wild swings of emotional atmosphere. When the parents are sober or drug free, there may be a feeling of normalcy, even of warmth and nurturing. But when the twisting of alcohol or drugs is at work, those same parents become unrecognizable; human decency and control take flight, and the child is left at the mercy of monsters. She knows her home to be a shambles; ashamed, she goes to great lengths to conceal the awfulness from friends, teachers, church members, and others.

The immoral home. Here the child is like a lily in a swamp: she grows up in the midst of moral slime. She sees and hears adulthood at its lowest level.

My heart broke one day in a local department store when I saw firsthand such a home in operation. My daughter and I were in the lingerie department; also among the racks were a scruffy-looking man and a much younger woman, obviously a foreigner. With them and addressing the man as "Daddy," but being profoundly ignored, were two little boys; the older of the two could not have been more than six or seven. The woman, loudly and lewdly assisted by suggestions from the man, was choosing some very scanty lingerie items. Tagging along behind, both little boys heard and saw it all, and, of course, that would have been only the beginning of the foulness they endured in their father's illicit relationship.

Some years ago I had the privilege to serve as a surrogate mother to a precious girl from an immoral home. My heart yearned for her to see what Christian womanhood and home life were meant to be, in contrast to what she knew by experience. Her mother was a prostitute. The girl did not know, of course, who her father was; her youthful existence had been a beautiless kaleidoscope. As she entered her teens, her mother was determined that the daughter follow in her footsteps; only by the grace of God was the girl preserved for the time when she would come to Bob Jones University. What a special trophy of God's grace! She ultimately met and married a fine young man with whom she established a Christian home. Needless to say, it was not easy for this girl's heart to escape the slime of her background. But she became a lovely example of one who mounts up on wounded wings.

The shattered home. Whatever the child's age when schism destroys the parents' marriage, her world is shaken, for the unity of mother and father is the emotional base upon which her life stands. When divorce occurs, security is replaced by uncertainty; peacefulness is exchanged for churning unease. The child's mind fills with questions about the parents' relationship; she seeks reasons for its rupture. In searching for answers, she is plagued by the shadow of guilt, feeling that she is herself somehow to blame. There also comes to her mind a hulking vulture of doubt about future marital stability in her own life.

The abusive home. There are multiple ways to slap a child in the face. Abuse may be physical, mental, or emotional, or it may occur in various combinations of these. The child of an abusive home is actually safest when she is away from that home. Within its walls she may suffer unimaginable cruelties. One young woman told me of having her mother shove her head into the toilet and flush it as punishment for minor offenses. Another related a youth interspersed with terror-filled times when her father would stand her against a wall and outline her body with bullets fired from his revolver. The tales of horror go on and on; they are being written daily in innocent-looking homes in every community. Children in such homes live in constant fear of angering a parent, cowering lest terrifying retribution be taken. They are too young to realize that there is no real triggering of the violence; the violence dwells within the twisted adults themselves, ever smoldering, ever ready to burst into searing flames.

The incestuous home. Here lurks sick sexuality: the uncle, brother, or cousin who should value the girl, instead violates her body, mind, and soul; the father or grandfather, who should tenderly protect and nurture, instead ravages her entire being. Trust becomes terror; innocence turns to distorted, horrid, illicit knowledge. The self of a child in such a home is stomped with hobnail boots.

Understanding the Pain

Can anyone from a normal home understand the endless, searing pain inflicted by a hurtful home? Can she comprehend the heartbreak which comes when a child's innocence and love are betrayed by those who brought her into the world? *God knows*. He understands. Contemplate Psalm 57:4, in which the Lord moved the psalmist to write,

> *My soul is among lions: and I lie even among them that are set on fire, even the sons of men, whose teeth are spears and arrows, and their tongue a sharp sword.*

How graphically that might echo the heart cry of one whose childhood was marred by home hurts in whatever form.

Wolves in Sheep's Clothing

The tragic point which must be made in this book is that *all of the horrible homes described exist within the Christian community*. Not one of them, of course, is advertised for what it is. Instead, it is carefully disguised by respectable titles and positions, cloaked by public religiosity. A woman who sings beautifully every Sunday in the church choir may on weekdays scream like a banshee at her children. The man who regularly leads in praying for missionaries may ridicule a son's calling to preach. The Sunday school teacher who thrills her listeners with in-depth studies of the book of Esther may excel in put-downs of a daughter she considers unworthy of her. The smiling usher who graciously bows as he hands the offering plate down the rows may be a secret alcoholic. The deacon who is most often called upon to read Scripture may quote Bible verses as he batters his wife and children. The preacher whose sermons are marvels of persuasive construction may be sexually abusing his ten-year-old daughter. Shocking? Yes. Revolting? Assuredly. Sin? Definitely.

During his earthly ministry Jesus spoke most harshly to those whose religious exteriors masked wretched interiors.

> *Ye are like unto whited sepulchres, which indeed appear beautiful outward, but are within full of dead men's bones, and of all uncleanness. Even so ye also outwardly appear righteous unto men, but within ye are full of hypocrisy and iniquity.*
>
> *Matthew 23:27-28*

Because the church today contains such masqueraders both in pulpit and pew, it is much like long-ago Israel as seen in Isaiah's thundering description.

> *The whole head is sick, and the whole heart faint. From the sole of the foot even unto the head there is no soundness in it; but wounds, and bruises, and putrifying sores: they have not been closed, neither bound up, neither mollified with ointment.*
>
> *Isaiah 1:5-6*

The wounds, bruises, and putrefaction mar the church; they make her robe of righteousness a stained, tattered thing. But the pictured whole also must be seen in individual human terms: numberless children robbed of childhood's joy and beauty; tender, helpless youngsters violated in their bodies, minds, and hearts.

> *The spirit of a man will sustain his infir-*
> *mity; but a wounded spirit who can bear?*
> *Proverbs 18:14*

Jesus Christ also directed special reproach and warning toward those who offend children.

> *And whosoever shall offend one of these lit-*
> *tle ones that believe in me, it is better for*
> *him that a millstone were hanged about*
> *his neck, and he were cast into the sea.*
> *Mark 9:42*

A Shattering Nest

What lasting influence can a harmful home background have upon a child—upon that child grown to adulthood? The effects are numerous and varied; they reach into virtually every area of the victim's life. We can liken a harmful home background to a *malformed nest.*

The proper home nest is placed, built, and tended for the purpose of protection. The hurtful home violates that principle in every aspect.

- Its careless placement exposes the helpless young to the elements.

- Its weak materials and shoddy construction threaten their falling through.

- Its tending is empty mockery.

A good home nest also contains a clean, clear, well-polished mirror in which the nestling gets an accurate picture of her own worth, in which she sees goodness in others, from which she perceives hope and encouragement in the surrounding world. The harmful home, too, holds up a mirror from which the young form their judgments, but the mirror has been shattered. The little one looks into a broken surface; bits and pieces of glass stuck at odd angles into the nest's walls make it impossible to catch a true reflection of anything. Instead, the developing resident sees herself and all of life in a confused, distorted parody of reality.

The shattered mirror of a treacherous home nest also does more; with its sharp edges and jagged points it scrapes, cuts, and gashes. The wounds, though invisible, are real, and scars remain through all succeeding days. The young soul is left with wounded wings on which to fly the winds of life.

CHAPTER THREE
THE WOUNDS

Many negative characteristics may cling to the human product of a hurtful home. The origin of those characteristics may not even be recognized by the one who bears them. Her unawareness makes it understandable that those around her might not think to look beneath her surface as loved one, friend, or acquaintance but simply react negatively to her unpleasant characteristic or behavior.

Most of the negative characteristics are attitudes and emotions; for scars, like wounds, can be internal and remain raw. At times the pain from them seems to be lessening; at other times it may throb so intensely as to threaten sanity or survival. The inward scars may take various forms.

Characteristics

Regret. Long after tears have dried on cheeks, they continue to fall within the heart. "If only" echoes endlessly in the mind. The real home stands grotesquely, a stark skeleton etched against the brightness of yearning. The words of Proverbs 14:13 are a daily reality.

> *Even in laughter the heart is sorrowful; and the end of that mirth is heaviness.*

Besides regret over deficiences of and damages from the home itself, the survivor may also regret her own negative reactions—words and behavior which did nothing to alleviate the situation, but rather may have intensified it. It is proper to recognize one's own contribution to past horrors and seek God's forgiveness while also seeking His healing.

> *The troubles of my heart are enlarged: O bring thou me out of my distresses. Look upon mine affliction and my pain; and forgive all my sins.*
>
> *Psalm 25:17-18*

Regret's scar burns anew at unexpected times—in a friend's joyful telling of some childhood incident; at the magazine advertisement which pictures a family gathered around a holiday table; during a drive through a quiet neighborhood at dusk (the windows of houses framing normalcy); at the fast-food establishment in whose play yard young mothers sit smiling upon their cavorting children.

Frustration. Along with regret may be the desire to undo the past—to break free. There is a sense of being bound by invisible cords; struggle only makes them tighten and cut.

The victim may flail persistently against the ever-looming past, making it a scapegoat for every present shortcoming.

Feeling cheated. There is a tendency in human make-up to look around oneself—to exaggerate the positives in others' selves and settings while minimizing one's own. That tendency is reinforced in a person with memories of a flawed childhood. Her emotional emptiness creates a cavern in which others' apparently normal, happy childhoods resound overloud. The comparison is painful, and the product of a shattered home feels cheated of something which should have been hers. As one young woman put it, "I always wished I were someone else, in a different family with different parents." The sense of having been shortchanged can become a constant irritant.

Emotional starvation. A child's emotional needs are enormous. When they are not met by those who should supply them, her inner self experiences hunger pangs as real as anything in the physical realm. Just as is the case with a child whose nutritional needs are denied, so it is with the one whose emotional needs go unmet: the effect is either emaciated weakness or bulging deformities.

Damaged self-image. When a child meets rebuffs instead of hugs, when she is hurt rather than helped, when weakness is violated rather than protected, when her developing being is kicked instead of kissed, the result is self-denigration and guilt. The bewildered youngster feels that there must be something wrong with her—some flaw or failure causing the chaos.

The sense of being a misfit, a disappointment, a living impossibility, remain long after the victim leaves childhood. Pictures speak louder than words; a hurtful home relentlessly pictures the child to herself as *unworthy* of others' warmth and acceptance.

Bitterness. Any of the previously named characteristics can harden into bitterness—against people, against circumstances, against life, against God. This response not only draws down the corners of the mouth and puts hardness in the glance but also eats internally like an acid and flows out scaldingly in spirit and speech.

Anger. Whereas bitterness is acidic, anger is inflammatory. The helpless ire kindled in the victim's heart toward the core of home may sweep into ever wider circles until she withdraws from or strikes out against all of society.

All the characteristics described above are natural human responses to childhood crippling; they carry on into adulthood as an emotional wing dragging. The intense, lingering struggle against memories and angry reactions to them is akin to that expressed in Psalm 56:2:

Mine enemies would daily swallow me up:
for they be many that fight against me.

Regret, frustration, the feeling of being cheated, emotional starvation, a damaged self-image, bitterness, and anger are characteristics of the internal self; they are not in themselves readily identifiable by others. Indeed, they are often disguised—redirected either intentionally or subconsciously.

Manifestations

Because wounds from a hurtful home pervade the inner being, they are impossible to hide completely; their surface manifestations, however, may cause puzzlement. The most common markers are the following.

Perfectionism. At first glance, this obsessiveness may seem an irrelevant or minor thing. But perfectionism makes its owner as well as others miserable. It is a carry-over from youthful days when every effort met displeasure, when no matter how carefully the child guarded words and actions and regardless of how diligently she strove, nothing could win the word of approval, the embrace, the freedom from assault. Moving from childhood into adulthood, the individual may clutch, as a child does a bedraggled doll, a pitiful striving to prove herself.

Distrust. It is not difficult to understand how severe, prolonged disappointment would foster distrust. From earliest years the child learned that those most greatly trusted proved to be most traitorous. Almost inevitably, the immature mind and heart extends self-protective distrust to all. It is not that she does not *want* to trust; rather, her memories of disappointment or terror hold her in bondage.

Fearfulness. Having been terrorized throughout childhood, the grown woman may be unable to free herself of a craven spirit. There may be a generalized fearfulness toward life, or fear may be crystallized into one or more of the various phobias. Very often horrific recollections suppressed during daylight hours invade the dark as nightmares; for instance, memories of incest may dominate dreams in the form of snakes.

Over- or under-achievement. Some who come from homes in which nurturing was deficient go through life driving themselves unmercifully. They are compelled toward outstanding accomplishment as if at last it might win acceptance from unapproving parents. Conversely, others react to their home's deficiency by assuming their own personal deficiency, consistently coming up short in effort and accomplishment.

Aggressiveness. Just as the little girl learned to duck the slap or evade the lecherous groping, when grown to womanhood she may manifest a spirit of constant fight-or-flight. In order to survive her young years she had to use her wits, and she finds it difficult to lay them aside now. She keeps her emotional boxing gloves on.

Self-distancing. While yearning for the love denied her in childhood, the home-hurt adult nevertheless finds it difficult or impossible to give or receive love. Emotional channels which would normally carry the life-giving supply of love can be blocked.

Parasitic relationships. In some ways the opposite of an inability to have closeness, this manifestation may appear to be the giving and receiving of love. But it is a sad, sick parody. Having been denied the close-holding of parents, the product of a wounding home fastens upon some person as a love or friendship object with unhealthy intensity, demanding sustenance.

After I had spoken about harmful home backgrounds in a seminar, a lady from the audience waited to speak to me privately. With trembling lips she told of her daughter-in-law, who personified a parasitic relationship. The young woman had first pursued this lady's son, pressuring him into marriage with the intensity of her need for him. Once married, she drew him more and more apart from normal life and relationships—cutting him off from friends, from family, and from the ministry call—all because she demanded his total focus as a means of sustaining her own being. I use the word *parasitic* to underline the ultimate effect of such a spirit: sucking life out of the host.

Eating disorders. In reaching for acceptance, comfort, and love, a home-hurt individual may find food the most readily available substitute for humanity's warmth. The misuse of food can take various forms: gluttony, anorexia, or bulimia. These are particularly prevalent in Christian circles because the use of alcohol or drugs is shunned as being clearly sinful. The wounded one may try to fill her emotional needs by stuffing herself with food. She may attempt to make herself as ugly on the outside as she feels on the inside. Conversely, she may so intently strive for affection-getting beauty that she starves herself to skin and bone lest she be "fat." Or, finally, she may binge on food, filling her stomach as a means of comforting her empty heart, and then react to the guilt of overeating by forcing herself to vomit.

Physical maladies

Because God created us wonderfully integrated beings, that which affects one part of us ultimately affects other parts. Physical problems particularly appear in those who deny the reality of or sublimate reactions to their painful past experiences. If a sufferer suppresses in herself emotional response and rational examination, she does something akin to capping a volcano: she redirects the eruption. There must be release of some sort: pain's lava denied in mind and heart eventually explodes in the body. There are any number of resulting maladies which may plague such a person: debilitating headaches, chronic insomnia, ulcers, glaucoma, rheumatoid arthritis.

Promiscuity

Sexual looseness marks particularly the child of an incestuous home, but it can also result from any of the hurtful home types. For the sake of specifics, I will use the incestuous home as the example.

When a girl is taught in her most impressionable years and with agonizing clarity that she is trash, a physical object unworthy of protection and care by those who should treasure her, she may not only accept that valuation of herself but also extend what she knows of sexual depravity in her father, uncle, grandfather, or cousin to an impression of all men in general. She then may personally expand her participation in the perceived universal pattern of wickedness, all the while hating both herself and her illicit partners. Various studies show a high incidence of incest in the home backgrounds of prostitutes.

So it is that the reflecting shards of a marred home nest present to its progeny cruel, distorted images of themselves, of others, and of life. Whether the distortions be few or many in that vital mirror, the result is real, the hurts deep, the confusion devastating.

Critical Recognition

Does one of the scarrings just discussed torment you personally? While it is wrong to blame every aberrant behavior, character shortcoming, or personality flaw on your past, it is also wrong to deny or ignore it. God's Word repeatedly tells us to "lay aside" or "cast off" clinging bits of darkness which hamper our testimony or hurt others.

How do you discern such things? How do you recognize your personal scar complications? Seek God's offered enlightenment. Ask Him to show you those things formed by and retained from your past which contribute to your wing dragging today. He will do so for the sake of your good and His glory.

While it is necessary to discuss the carry-overs from hurtful home backgrounds, *enumerating them in no way is meant to excuse having persisted in them.* The purpose is to define, to identify—whether for self-recognition by a hitherto unrecognizing victim or for compassionate understanding from an onlooker.

The signs of crippling presented in this chapter can and should be purged from the life. Debilitation can be replaced by wholeness as the wounded one chooses to submit to the Great Physician's hand.

The point of this writing, therefore, is not to dwell upon time past, the home's hurtfulness, or its particular wounds. It is not simply to awaken self-pitying or humanitarian tears. The prayerful purpose is to *redirect the focus of mind, heart, spirit, and life.* That focus must be shifted from the woundings below and lifted heavenward.

There above us is the great God who is "high and lifted up" but yet in matchless love hovers close, responding to our hurt and our fear with the promise of His healing and His protective, enabling strength. Seeing Him, we can cease from our useless dust examination and say,

> *How excellent is thy lovingkindness, O*
> *God! therefore the children of men put their*
> *trust under the shadow of thy wings.*
> *Psalm 36:7*

CHAPTER FOUR
THE CHOICE FOR HEALING

For the sake of clarity and focus, at this point I am going to change from the generalized approach of the earlier chapters to a specific one. The remaining chapters will be addressed directly to that one whose wing wounds need God's healing.

No matter how destructive your childhood home may have been, no matter how cruel the wounds you experienced from it, healing can take place. God not only *wants* to heal; He and He alone, the Great Physician, has the ability to heal home hurts.

Deep in the recesses of a wounded one's mind and heart may lie an unspoken ethical association: if one has been *hurt while helpless,* she may reasonably expect to be *healed while helpless.* But healing is not, indeed *cannot* be, automatic. It is not something imposed from without; it must begin from within, as we who have been victimized by hurtful homes *choose* to move from victimization to victory.

Healing's Requirements

The wounds from a hurtful home background can be likened to physical hurts: a scratch or a bruise heals readily; a stab wound or a broken limb does not. Serious hurts demand (1) a physician, (2) treatment, and (3) time. All three of these are available to the wing-wounded Christian woman. But in heart hurts as in body hurts, the injured one *must choose* to be helped; she must pursue healing.

The Struggle-Filled Choice

Those who are privileged to look back on a normal, happy childhood cannot comprehend the enormous struggle which may take place at this point of choice. One of the deepest gougings in a home wound is the sense of its indelibleness or eternality. The uglies of the past are so awful, and their pain so deeply agonizing, that they seem permanently imbedded, an aching but irremovable part of one's being.

Blinding and Binding

The hurting human spirit and an antagonistic Satan may (unwittingly on the part of the victim) join hands at this strategic juncture. Our archenemy wants the shatterings of the past to do two things: *blind* and *bind*. Tear-filled eyes staring fixedly at home's splintered mirror can *blind* us to God's love and His goodness; they can also *bind* us so tightly to the past as to cripple us in the present. But that blinding and binding power can be broken.

Blinding. Parents are the earliest and most consequential molders of a child's God concept. Unfortunately, the picture of God presented by some parents is sadly flawed. It must be replaced by an *accurate* view of Him. The fact that a human parent is careless, treacherous, cruel, or perverted does not mean that our Heavenly Father is similarly callous.

The Bible tells us that God not only loves; He *is* love—its essence and its source. At every point where human love falters or fails, God's love shines with ineffable purity and immeasurable depth. Consider only a few of those points. Let's look at four *F's* of human love in contrast with divine.

First, human love *fluctuates* according to presumed deserving and in intensity of action: the "good" child may be cuddled; the cross child, slapped. It also fluctuates according to the parent's physical, mental, emotional, and spiritual state at the moment.

There is no change in God's love for His beloved. As it is true of Christ the Son, so it is true of God the Father—He is "the *same* yesterday, today, and forever." Divine love, then, is *constant,* emanating

> *. . . from the Father of lights, with whom is*
> *no variableness, neither shadow of turning.*
> James 1:17

Second, human parental love *falters.* There are some barriers, whether in the child or in the parent, that are too strong for natural affection to overcome. The parent who herself came from an unloving home may have in her psyche, deeply entrenched, a restraint against giving affection to or receiving it from her own children.

Divine love is *unfaltering.*

> *Who shall separate us from the love of*
> *Christ? shall tribulation, or distress, or perse-*
> *cution, or famine, or nakedness, or peril, or*
> *sword? For I am persuaded, that neither*

> *death, nor life, nor angels, nor principali-*
> *ties, nor powers, nor things present, nor*
> *things to come, Nor height, nor depth, nor*
> *any other creature, shall be able to separate*
> *us from the love of God, which is in Christ*
> *Jesus our Lord.*
>
> Romans 8:35, 38-39

Third, parents' earthly love *fails*. It can fail at one or many points along the path of the child's growing up. Perhaps it fails at one of the earliest points, perception. The parent fails to understand the nature of the offspring and so does not respond with positive nurturing.

God's love *never fails*.

> *The Lord hath appeared of old unto me,*
> *saying, Yea, I have loved thee with an ever-*
> *lasting love: therefore with lovingkindness*
> *have I drawn thee.*
>
> Jeremiah 31:3

Fourth, humans not only fluctuate, falter, and fail in their love but also sometimes utterly *forsake* a child. Heartbreaking stories of physically abandoned children appear often in newspapers or magazines. The forsaking may be not physical but emotional: though physical provision continues, affectionate care does not.

Divine love *holds its child in an unchanging, unrelaxing embrace.*

> *Can a woman forget her sucking child, that*
> *she should not have compassion on the son*
> *of her womb? yea, they may forget, yet will*
> *I not forget thee.*
>
> Isaiah 49:15

It is clear throughout Scripture that the character and care of God far surpass those of our earthly parents. Let the Word's assurances defeat Satan's efforts to *blind* you to the beauty, strength, and eternality of God's love.

Binding. There must likewise be a willed decision against being bound by and to sorrows of the past. This is a juncture at which scriptural instruction and secular "support" groups sharply diverge. The latter create an atmosphere in which detailing one's own hurtful experiences and listening to others do the same with theirs is in itself meant to be a cure. But a wound must be not only *uncovered* but also *treated.* Indeed, repeated uncoverings without treatment can worsen the wound through exposure to infection.

It is imperative that we move emotionally far enough away from our wounds to see them objectively. That is difficult, but for the Christian it lies well within possibility. Changing the perspective is a matter of choosing the objectivity which comes from God's Word.

Subjective (emotional) consideration brings only a deepening sense of hopelessness. Objective examination by Scripture assures the hurting heart that there is hope.

A hurtful home, certainly, makes a negative contribution *to one's quality of life and being; but the contribution is not a* condemnation *to live at the mercy of its negatives.* Any seeming permanence and inevitability of its consequences are false: *nothing* need remain unchanged when God's grace and power are brought to bear upon it. Satan wants to bind us to yesterday's pain. God wants to *free* us from it.

For born-again Christians, each of whom has access to God's grace and power, the star of hope shines even in the darkest sky.

> *Now the God of hope fill you with all joy*
> *and peace in believing, that ye may abound*
> *in hope, through the power of the Holy*
> *Ghost.*
>
> *Romans 15:13*

In the strength of that divine hope, let us move on to some other truths necessary to an understanding of hurting and healing.

Suffering

The question which rises so often in the mind of the home-wounded woman is *why?* Why did I have to endure hurt? Why do any of us have to suffer, anyway? Would a loving God really allow all the cruel, senseless pain which fills our world?

The Bible has much to say about suffering. First, it tells us that human life in general is filled with difficulties.

> *Yet man is born unto trouble, as the sparks*
> *fly upward.*
>
> *Job 5:7*

> *Man that is born of a woman is of few*
> *days, and full of trouble.*
>
> *Job 14:1*

Suffering, then, is universal—part and parcel of the human condition. Yet in considering personal hurts, the Christian may be tempted to protest further, noting that "man" is a generic term. That unregenerate, *sinful* mankind suffers makes sense of a sort; but what about *good* people—specifically, *Christians*—those who are supposed to be special to and beloved of God? Long ago God spoke clearly and encouragingly about the subject.

Many are the afflictions of the righteous:
but the Lord delivereth him out of them all.
                                                    Psalm 34:19

We must simply accept the fact that Christians are not exempt from any of earth's woes: Jesus Christ Himself said, speaking to those who loved Him most and served Him best,

In the world ye shall have tribulation.
                                                    John 16:33

Believers, then, are not *exempt from* but rather are meant to be *examples in* tribulation. Even before healing is fully yours, know assuredly that God is now using, or will in the future use, the *example* of your pain and its healing in one of two ways: as an encouragement to another believer struggling with pain or as a magnet to draw some unsaved onlooker to salvation. He or she, recognizing the depth of your hurt and identifying with it through his own, can awaken to the *healing* made possible by Jesus Christ.

Suffering's Cause

The basic cause of suffering is sinfulness. All mankind was plunged into sin when, in the Garden of Eden, Adam and Eve believed Satan's lie and ate the fruit which God had forbidden. From the bliss of Eden they moved to the blight of evil and its sufferings.

The truth of humanity's sinfulness is daily lived out all around us: men and women break God's law at every turn, leaving behind them a trail of tragedy. The awfulness of the sinful human condition cannot be more accurately pictured or more fully seen than as it is presented in the book of Romans. Read thoughtfully through the following passage.

When they knew God, they glorified him not as God, neither were thankful; but became vain in their imaginations, and their foolish heart was darkened. Professing themselves to be wise, they became fools, And changed the glory of the uncorruptible God into an image made like to corruptible man, and to birds, and fourfooted beasts, and creeping things. Wherefore God also gave them up to uncleanness through the lusts of their own hearts, to dishonor their own bodies between themselves: Who changed the truth of God into a lie, and worshipped and served the creature more than the Creator, who is blessed for ever. Amen. For this cause God gave them up unto vile affections: for even their women did change the natural use into that which is against nature: And likewise also the men, leaving the natural use of the woman, burned in their lust one toward another; men with men working that which is unseemly, and receiving in themselves that recompense of their error which was meet. And even as they did not like to retain God in their knowledge, God gave them over to a reprobate mind, to do those things which are not convenient; Being filled with all unrighteousness, fornication, wickedness, covetousness, maliciousness; full of envy, murder, debate, deceit, malignity; whisperers, Backbiters, haters of God, despiteful, proud, boasters, inventors of evil things, disobedient to parents, Without understanding, covenantbreakers, without natural affection, implacable, unmerciful: Who knowing the judgment of God, that they which commit such things are worthy of death, not only do the same, but have pleasure in them that do them.

Romans 1:21-32

Human suffering comes not only because of personal sinfulness but also innocently as the inevitable result of others' wickedness.

The "Christianity" Complication

At this point some hurting reader will respond, "All that perpetration of wickedness might be expected from the unsaved; but the one who mistreated and betrayed me *claims the title of 'Christian.'* " That protesting heart cry cannot really be *answered;* it can only be addressed.

First, "Christianity" can be a surface-only thing: language, appearance, and church involvement mask many a heart that knows nothing of cleansing by Christ's blood.

Second, every born-again believer is constantly faced with choosing between right and wrong; though he *should,* of course, choose the former, he all too often chooses the latter. Because he is a lifelong resident in a human body, he *is capable of any sin.* Apart from Jesus Christ, the Son of God, there has never been anyone who lived without sin. Even some heroes of the Faith made sinful choices: Abraham was a liar, Moses was a murderer, the psalmist David an adulterer.

Third, a Christian's conscience can become desensitized. Sin has a numbing effect; if it is not quickly confessed and repented of, it remains as a callous on the soul. As it thickens, conviction decreases. Continued sin thus creates the "seared conscience" mentioned in I Timothy 4:2.

Whoever it was who hurt you, whether he or she claimed to be a Christian, the underlying reason for your mistreatment was *sin*. By making sinful choices, this person entered into league with Satan, the destroyer.

Sin's Conqueror

While we must acknowledge Satan to be powerful, cruel, and subtle, that recognition should serve only as a springboard for confidence as we remind ourselves that

> *. . . greater is he that is in you, than he that is in the world.*
>
> I John 4:4

Satan's desire is to keep you bound in the chains of the past so that you will be ineffective in your own person and unable to fulfill the ministry in and to the Body of Christ which God has planned for you. If you submit to that binding, you become a trophy of his treachery. In order to thwart Satan's desire and cooperate with God's purpose, we are told to

> *. . . submit yourselves therefore to God. Resist the devil, and he will flee from you.*
>
> James 4:7

Satan's hold on your yesterdays does not extend to your today or tomorrow. He is a *defeated* opponent; whatever his grasp, it can be loosened by the all-powerful hand of God. We can pray with the psalmist,

> *Be merciful unto me, O God, be merciful unto me: for my soul trusteth in thee: yea, in the shadow of thy wings will I make my refuge, until these calamities be overpast.*
>
> Psalm 57:1

Consider the God to whom we are to submit as we resist the Devil, in the shadow of whose wings we may take refuge—that mighty One who dwells not only in eternity, maintaining and directing all of His creation, but also within the believer in the Person of the Holy Spirit. Let the Bible speak to your heart of the two characteristics of God which can particularly engender hope and encourage you to choose His healing: His power and His compassion.

God's Power

There is no limit to God's power. That is the meaning of the word *omnipotent:* "*all*-powerful." Go back to the opening chapters of Genesis. Revisit with awed concentration the days in which God spoke into existence everything of, in, and around our planet earth. Let your heart focus upon what God says Himself about His power.

The Lord of hosts hath sworn, saying, Surely as I have thought, so shall it come to pass; and as I have purposed, so shall it stand.
Isaiah 14:24

For the Lord of hosts hath purposed, and who shall disannul it? and his hand is stretched out, and who shall turn it back?
Isaiah 14:27

To whom then will ye liken me, or shall I be equal? saith the Holy One. Lift up your eyes on high, and behold who hath created these things, that bringeth out their host by number: he calleth them all by names by the greatness of his might, for that he is strong in power; not one faileth.
Isaiah 40:25-26

Psalm 107, which catalogs various aspects of God's goodness and wonderful works in human lives, contains the following:

> *Then they cried unto the Lord in their*
> *trouble, and he saved them out of their dis-*
> *tresses. He brought them out of darkness*
> *and the shadow of death, and brake their*
> *bands in sunder.*
>
> *Psalm 107:13-14*

How wonderful it is that the God of all might—Heavenly Father to each blood-born Christian—does not sit aloof, isolated in His majesty and insulated from our needs.

God's Compassion

Compassion is empathetic care—"feeling-in" with another's pain. That is exactly what God extends to us wounded ones as He identifies with our hurt through the hurt which Christ experienced. Consider Zechariah's compelling prophecy concerning Christ.

> *And one shall say unto him, What are*
> *these wounds in thine hands? Then he*
> *shall answer, Those with which I was*
> *wounded in the house of my friends.*
>
> *Zechariah 13:6*

God's great heart of love is hurt by our pain. He not only sees cruel actions which may be hidden from human observation; He also sees and feels the *results* of those actions—the tormented mind, the crushed heart.

> *For we have not an high priest which*
> *cannot be touched with the feeling of our*
> *infirmities.*
>
> *Hebrews 4:15*

As God *feels* our pain, so He responds with the promise of healing.

> *For I will restore health unto thee, and I will heal thee of thy wounds, saith the Lord.*
>
> Jeremiah 30:17

The psalmist expresses the intimacy of our Heavenly Father's concern for our sorrows in Psalm 56:8.

> *Thou tellest my wanderings: put thou my tears into thy bottle: are they not in thy book?*

Bible Examples

God does not stop with simply understanding and being touched by our plight. He also opens the way to our surmounting the painful past. He encourages us to set foot on that upward course by providing us with object lessons. Bending to us in His love, God gives to you and me pictures of those who have endured hurtful home backgrounds before us. Consider several.

Moses certainly could not be said to have grown up in a normal home. The three-month-old baby, first hidden among the bulrushes, went on to live in a mixed-up domestic ménage where his godly mother, denying the natural bond, went disguised as his nurse, while his heathen adoptive mother trained him in Egypt's court life.

Samuel was a young child (freshly weaned from his mother's breast) when he was removed from his natural home and placed in the temple. Too often in telling Samuel's story we dwell on its wonderful aspects while completely overlooking what it must have meant in human terms: "desertion" by his parents; a sterile, formal upbringing by a gluttonous priest who failed to curb the ungodliness of his own sons. Not very promising surroundings for one's tender childhood years!

We are not told at what age *Esther* was orphaned—only that she had become the ward of her cousin, Mordecai. Nor, to put it mildly, was her path to matrimony strewn with the roses of love's young dream.

Joseph's home background could be termed hurtful with a capital *H!* Parental favoritism, jealously competing mothers, resentful siblings, plottings and treachery—all must have kept the boy Joseph in a state of constant upset as he reeled back and forth from his father's coddling to everyone else's coldness.

In letters of the Apostle Paul to his ministry student, we learn that *Timothy* came from a home where his grandmother and his mother were Christians, but his father was not. Might the young preacher's timidity and frail health have resulted from an abusive father?

For each of the Bible characters mentioned, as for numberless other dwellers in humanity's frail shell, there doubtless were times when the psalmist's generalizing observations became personal.

> *I said in my haste, I am cut off from before*
> *thine eyes: nevertheless thou heardest the voice*
> *of my supplications when I cried unto thee.*
> *Psalm 31:22*

Now let us consider the consequences in the lives of these victims of impaired pasts. What effects can be seen in their spiritual stature and life accomplishments? They became character dwarfs and spiritual misfits, right? Wrong! Each one towers from the Bible's pages. All grew to be *giants of the Faith!* From a human standpoint, their home backgrounds should have produced failures. But contemplate how God, speaking through Jacob of Joseph, underscores the opposite.

> *Joseph is a fruitful bough, even a fruitful*
> *bough by a well; whose branches run over*
> *the wall: The archers have sorely grieved*
> *him, and shot at him, and hated him: But*
> *his bow abode in strength, and the arms of*
> *his hands were made strong by the hands*
> *of the mighty God of Jacob.*
>
> *Genesis 49:22-24*

What is said of Joseph could just as accurately be said of the rest: the marrings of home were not only sur-mounted; they were *used* by the great hand of God to create *richness* of self and service. The same can be accom-plished in you and me.

The Great Physician

Dear hurting, searching reader, let the force of these Bible examples kindle hope in your heart. Self-help is ineffective; psychiatric help is futile. We who bear wounds from childhood can well cry out with the psalmist,

> *Give us help from trouble: for vain is the*
> *help of man.*
>
> *Psalm 60:11*

Understand that *there is a Physician for your desperately wounded wings.* You are not condemned to drag about in the dust of defeat. The healing salve which proved effec-tive for Moses, Samuel, Esther, Joseph, Timothy, and numberless unnamed others continues freely available to us today. Will you reach out for it? Or will you refuse it, choosing instead to turn away and to continue in defeat? If you decide for the latter, the heart of your tender, loving Lord will grieve.

> *Is there no balm in Gilead; is there no phy-*
> *sician there? why then is not the health of*
> *the daughter of my people recovered?*
>
> Jeremiah 8:22

Malachi 4:2 draws a beautiful picture for us wounded ones:

> *But unto you that fear my name shall the*
> *Sun of righteousness arise with healing in*
> *his wings.*

The Great Challenge

Choose healing, my friend. Trust yourself to the care of that One who alone can heal your hurts and enable you to soar into the clear skies of wholeness.

Listen. Hear His blessed promise spoken directly to your heart.

> *Hast thou not known? hast thou not heard,*
> *that the everlasting God, the Lord, the Crea-*
> *tor of the ends of the earth, fainteth not,*
> *neither is weary? there is no searching of*
> *his understanding. He giveth power to the*
> *faint; and to them that have no might he*
> *increaseth strength. Even the youths shall*
> *faint and be weary, and the young men*
> *shall utterly fall: But they that wait upon*
> *the Lord shall renew their strength; they*
> *shall mount up with wings as eagles; they*
> *shall run, and not be weary; and they shall*
> *walk, and not faint.*
>
> Isaiah 40:28-31

Open your ears and your heart to His voice calling you upward. Let your entire being render a positive response.

Heal me, O Lord, and I shall be healed;
save me, and I shall be saved: for thou art
my praise.

Jeremiah 17:14

CHAPTER FIVE
THE HEALING PROCESS

The decision to choose healing is the necessary starting point for each of us whose wings have been hurt in the home nest. From that initial choice, an individual's course toward wholeness varies in distance and difficulty. Progress will be affected by a number of factors.

- The victim's personality and temperament
- The nature of the wound
- The length of time during and since the wounding
- Earlier reactions to the pain
- Specific interpersonal relationships

Let's briefly consider each of these factors.

The victim's personality and temperament. Like snowflakes, no two of us are alike. Our individualities color every aspect of our lives. That we respond differently to hurt, then, should come as no surprise. A woman who is a fighter by nature will be affected differently from one who crumples. One who expresses emotions outwardly may heal more readily than she who internalizes.

The nature of the wound. Each type of home hurt produces a wound having its own particular characteristics. For instance, the wound from a neglectful home may be mainly a vague, unfocused pain of regretful longing; the gash from a physically abusive home, on the other hand, can pulsate frustration and rage.

The length of time during and since the wounding. First, how long did the active hurt go on? A one-time incident of physical abuse wounds the heart differently from beatings lasting into the teen-age years. Second, how much time has elapsed since then? Time's passage may in itself induce healing. On the other hand, intervening years may act only as a nonmedicating cover, hiding continued festering.

Earlier reactions to the pain. Response to the hurt both originally and in the succeeding time span also affects healing. Was there angry verbal or physical reaction during the time pain was being inflicted? Has there since been denial with pretended peace? Have resentment and bitterness lain unpurged in the heart's depths? Has a reactive sinful lifestyle worsened the original wound?

Specific interpersonal relationships involved. Relationships are as varied as the individuals that form them. Original and continuing ties between the various people involved in your pain will influence healing's course.

The Treatment Explained

Healing cannot come instantly to injured wings; treatment must include certain steps:

- Protecting feathers have to be pulled aside, allowing the wound to be seen.

- Dirt and possible putrefaction must be removed from the broken flesh.
- Ointment must be applied to soothe and to protect the wound during the healing process.
- Broken bones have to be set and splinted.
- Tight, shrunken muscles must gradually be brought back into use.

None of the steps just mentioned is easy. Therefore, moving actively into the healing process demands courage—perhaps more courage than you feel you possess. At this crucial juncture you must begin the *leaning* and *leaving,* so necessary in the healing process: *you must lean* on the strong arm of the Lord and *leave* the weight of your heart on His. Initiate the practice by claiming the following passages.

The Lord is nigh unto them that are of a broken heart.
　　　　　　　　　　　Psalm 34:18

For the Lord shall be thy confidence, and shall keep thy foot from being taken.
　　　　　　　　　　　Proverbs 3:26

I sought the Lord, and he heard me, and delivered me from all my fears.
　　　　　　　　　　　Psalm 34:4

The angel of the Lord encampeth round about them that fear him, and delivereth them.
　　　　　　　　　　　Psalm 34:7

The eyes of the Lord are upon the righteous, and his ears are open unto their cry.
　　　　　　　　　　　Psalm 34:15

*The righteous cry, and the Lord heareth,
and delivereth them out of all their troubles.*
Psalm 34:17

*Through God we shall do valiantly: for he
it is that shall tread down our enemies.*
Psalm 60:12

*I can do all things through Christ which
strengtheneth me.*
Philippians 4:13

Memorize these verses. Cling to their promise of deliverance as you begin the process of healing.

The Treatment Experienced

Prescription Capsule #1—pull aside the feathers. It will be difficult to remove the covering and expose the wound. But it must be done. It is essential that you look squarely at your hurt, no matter how fearsome the examination, no matter how foul the wound. *Name* your wounding.

- incest
- physical abuse
- mental abuse
- alcoholism
- rejection
- desertion
- betrayal
- other

Depending on the length of time you have fought to *hide* the wound, you may find it necessary to move slowly through the naming steps.

1. Name it—specifically—*aloud* to yourself.
2. Name it—again, specifically—*aloud* to God.

3. Name it to a trustworthy friend or counselor.

Each of the three steps in the naming process is necessary. The wound is real. It is there. It has been affecting and continues to affect you and your life. The wound must be uncovered or it can never really be healed.

Naming the wound aloud to yourself may seem deceptively easy. But in cases where wounds have been especially grievous and repulsive, putting a name to the horror can be excruciating: you will be pulling feathers out of dried, hardened blood. The effort may make you feel physically ill as you are swept into technicolor memories of the experiences you so yearn to forget. That is a normal reaction. Nevertheless, persevere. Look beyond the present exacerbated hurt to the eventual healing. Name your wounding until you no longer shrink, nauseated, at the naming.

Why is it necessary to name your hurt so specifically? Because until your wound is brought into the realm of thought, speech, and action, it remains in that of emotion, a compartment of the human self which cannot be *directly* changed or medicated.

The second step, speaking aloud to name your hurt to God, may likewise come only after a struggle. But the needfulness of this step can be seen in the psalmist's words:

> *I was dumb with silence, I held my peace,*
> *even from good; and my sorrow was stirred.*
> *My heart was hot within me; while I was*
> *musing the fire burned: then spake I with*
> *my tongue.*
>
> *Psalm 39:2-3*

> *I will say unto God my rock, Why hast
> thou forgotten me? why go I mourning be-
> cause of the oppression of the enemy?*
> *Psalm 42:9*

> *I cried unto the Lord with my voice; with
> my voice unto the Lord did I make my sup-
> plication. I poured out my complaint before
> him; I showed before him my trouble.*
> *Psalm 142:1-2*

While the Bible recognizes and mentions emotions—joy, sorrow, and anger, for example—God's instructions for self-control, obedience, and godly living focus upon the aspects of our being which are within our ability to control: thought and action. He never makes emotion itself the channel of change. Perhaps the most succinct expression of this truth is found in Joshua 1:8.

> *This book of the law shall not depart out of
> thy mouth; but thou shalt meditate therein
> day and night, that thou mayest observe to
> do according to all that is written therein:
> for then thou shalt make thy way prosper-
> ous, and then thou shalt have good success.*

Notice the three emphases of the above passage. First, God's Word is to be the core of the believer's life, the irreplaceable basis for spiritual success *regardless of feelings*. Second, we are to focus active thought upon the Word throughout every day and in every season of life *regardless of feelings*. Third, the purpose of that constant mental focus is to conform our actions to the Bible's commands *regardless of feelings*.

A second Scripture passage indicates that it is victory over thought rather than emotion which is decisive in the battle for healing.

> *For though we walk in the flesh, we do not*
> *war after the flesh: (for the weapons of our*
> *warfare are not carnal, but mighty through*
> *God to the pulling down of strong holds;)*
> *casting down imaginations, and every high*
> *thing that exalteth itself against the knowl-*
> *edge of God, and bringing into captivity*
> *every thought to the obedience of Christ.*
> *II Corinthians 10:3-5*

Note, again, that our feelings do not exempt us from this command.

Sometimes there is a sense that God may be surprised, shocked, or revolted by our wound's uncovering. Oh no, my friend. He has known all about it, and He has hurt with your hurt from the beginning. He has been patiently waiting for you to tire of your denials; to weary of your attempted disguises; to turn from your misdirected gropings for help; to run, at last, into His arms and weep out your anguish on His breast.

Job, that classic sufferer of old, voiced his most extreme agonies to God.

> *My soul is weary of my life; I will leave my*
> *complaint upon myself; I will speak in the*
> *bitterness of my soul.*
> *Job 10:1*

Job goes on through chapter eleven and indeed throughout the entire book to talk very honestly with his heavenly Father.

Having named your wounding aloud to yourself and to God, you will have succeeded in pulling aside the feathers that have covered but contaminated your wound. Now those feathers must be clipped back so that they will not complicate treatment: you need to name your hurt to a flesh-and-blood hearer.

> *Ointment and perfume rejoice the heart: so doth the sweetness of a man's friend by hearty counsel.*
>
> *Proverbs 27:9*

> *Iron sharpeneth iron: so a man sharpeneth the countenance of his friend.*
>
> *Proverbs 27:17*

When a human heart has borne a heavy burden, an important contributor to relief and release is a compassionate person who comes alongside. Putting it in simplest form, we need "someone with skin on."

Note, please, that verbalizing to a human listener does *not* mean to *go into details of your wounding.* Blow-by-blow discussion is not healthful either for you or for your listener.

When seeking a human hearer, exercise great care. Even more, undertake fervent prayer. Ask God to direct you to that special one whose ear and heart will be open, but whose mouth will be closed except to help and encourage you. Look and pray for the following qualities in your hearer-helper.

1. Spiritual maturity
2. Demonstrated, consistent compassion
3. Battle scars
4. A disciplined life
5. A guarded tongue

Warning

Do not be rushed in finding that right human listener. At this point I feel impressed to insert a specific warning. All the hurts being discussed in this book have to do with deep-seated emotions; some concern sexual matters. Where there is emotional emptiness or sexual complication in a woman's problem area, *there is extreme vulnerability*. It is important, therefore, that you *avoid* private counseling with a man. Satan is devastating the Christian community by using the counseling room as an anteroom to sexual immorality. According to Titus 2:4, it is *older women* who are to counsel younger ones. Do not be deceived into thinking that the devices of the Devil used against you in the past may not be used against you in the future. He would delight to pour into your wound the scalding acid of sinful entrapment.

Be aware, also, that a hastily chosen human hearer may actually worsen the wound by applying the wrong medication. Consider the apt word picture of Ecclesiastes 10:1.

*Dead flies cause the ointment of the apothe-
cary to send forth a stinking savor: so doth
a little folly him that is in reputation for
wisdom and honor.*

God knows the identity and location of that counselor *He* has for you, that human "apothecary" whose jar of spiritual ointment is fresh, clean, and effective. In His time, as you wait and pray patiently, He will call that one to your attention. Quite often God's chosen hearer-counselor is someone far removed from your own everyday setting. Physical distance and nonacquaintance with those involved may assist your free expression.

The Time Involved

Voicing your pain may be a one-time-only necessity; your listener's understanding and prayers may equip you to move on to the next step. It may be necessary, though, to have several sessions with her: the true extent of the wound, once revealed, may so shock and shake you that further progress is impossible at the moment. However, I do *not* advise the world's "support group" approach. Too often it becomes a get-nowhere, repeat-endlessly, feel-sorry-for-me morass from which progress is never made.

A Special Question

A further aspect to be considered with regard to naming your hurt is the question of whether you should confide in your husband or husband-to-be. That decision must be made with great care and after much prayer. As a general rule, I believe the answer is yes, for the reason that the past affects present and future attitudes, actions, and relationships. However, there are exceptions. Consider two examples.

A young woman who experienced sexual abuse in her childhood would probably be wiser to tell her fiancé than to shock and sadden him on their honeymoon by her inexplicable hesitancies or revulsion. There is the risk that he may not be able to put aside that revelation. Explaining the problem to him beforehand will test his character and spiritual strength. A failure on his part should be seen as a *rescue* from worse unsupportiveness ahead.

A woman in her sixties who has silently battled her memories of incest throughout thirty-odd years of marriage might more wisely carry the secret with her to the grave. As one such woman said to me, "I couldn't tell my husband. Even after all these years he'd kill my father for doing that to me."

This question—to reveal or not to reveal past hurts to someone who is emotionally related to you—is one of the numberless points along life's highway where there are no clearly lettered signposts. The type of hurt, the individual personalities, the circumstances, the time factors, and the nature of the relationships must all be weighed and God's clear direction sought.

But Why?

There is a final part to the feather-removal step: you must surrender your desire or demand *to understand*. When one of us wounded ones considers her hurt and its specifics, heart and mind unite in the tortured cry, *"Why? How could he or she or they do such a thing?" "Why* did I have to endure it?"* Our cry protests the unfairness of life itself.

You must give up the quest for an answer. It is a fruitless search for motivations hidden in the inscrutable depths of the human heart. The prophet Jeremiah gave the classic response long ago.

> *The heart is deceitful above all things, and*
> *desperately wicked: who can know it?*
> *Jeremiah 17:9*

Your wound and mine were caused by a human heart beating out of sync with the divine heart—perhaps masking its villainy even to the one in whose breast it beat. The human heart's murky depths and twisted contents are beyond *anyone's* understanding.

So, then, where human *comprehension* ends, we wounded ones must, by faith, undertake *commission*.

> *Commit thy way unto the Lord; trust also*
> *in him; and he shall bring it to pass.*
> *Psalm 37:5*

> *Trust in the Lord with all thine heart; and
> lean not unto thine own understanding.*
> Proverbs 3:5

> *Wait on the Lord, and keep his way, and he
> shall exalt thee to inherit the land: when
> the wicked are cut off, thou shalt see it.*
> Psalm 37:34

So clip away that small, final, but ever-irritating pin-feather of demand for explanation.

Prescription Capsule #2—remove dirt, debris, and putrefaction.

No wound can heal properly if it is not thoroughly cleansed. There may be several complicating bits of grime in your newly exposed hurt. Locate and remove them.

The dirt of denial. Very often this uncleanness is allowed to stay in the wound month after month, year after year, causing emotional festering. Why? Basically, I believe the answer is one or more of four types of *fear.* First, we may simply be afraid to face truth's rawness. Instead we close our eyes and our minds to it. But denial is a futile effort; it only delays the time when the dirt-produced infection becomes so bad that it erupts.

Second, we may deny the truth of our wounding through fear either *of* or *for* the offender. Some who victimize children make threats against the child or someone she loves if she should ever reveal the truth. Or her own imagination may still conjure childhood's irrational "what if" monsters. Then again, the restraining fear may be due to a distorted love for the offender.

Third, it is possible that we deny our hurt because of pride: we feel embarrassed that there continue to be effects in our lives from the wounding, perhaps after many years. We feel ashamed that the struggle continues long after it "should" have ceased.

Fourth, it may be easier to deny the truth than to expose our hearts to others' eyes. We fear their misunderstanding, their devaluation of us, their disbelief, their shock.

Fear is not sufficient reason to keep denial's dirt embedded in our torn hearts, where it prevents healing. We must look beyond these small, timid, trembling selves; look on and up to that Mighty One whom the prophet Isaiah saw "high and lifted up." We must listen beyond the frightened litany of our own hearts so that we can hear the Eternal Voice clarify our perspective:

> *I, even I, am he that comforteth you: who art thou, that thou shouldest be afraid of a man that shall die, and of the son of man which shall be made as grass; and forgettest the Lord thy maker, that hath stretched forth the heavens, and laid the foundations of the earth.*
>
> *Isaiah 51:12-13*

Whatever "man" it is we fear, within or without, we need to replace that freezing fear with the freeing fear of God. The great Creator God is the God of Truth. He wants truthfulness reflected in us, His born-again children, even when the truth may be painful.

The debris of guilt. Guilt's debris may be false or real. First, consider *false* guilt. Very often an adult who hurts a child physically, emotionally, or sexually eases his personal conscience by shifting blame. Consider a few of the common ploys.

> "Your dad and I did just fine together until you kids came along. . . ."

"I'm completely strung out under the pressure of keeping you clothed and fed. . . ."

"If you would learn to be a *good* girl, I wouldn't have to hit you. . . ."

"I really want to help you, you know; but you can't seem to get the message. . . ."

"This is what happens to little girls who are pretty like you. . . ."

When those and similar statements coming from the lips of *adults* (who are supposed to be *wise* and *right* in what they do) combine with the child's emotional devastation, it is no wonder she comes to believe the charges! The sharp-edged debris of false guilt worsens her wound's rawness.

If your wounds are kept raw by false guilt, close your ears to the remembered voices blaming you . . . blaming you. What they say *is not true.* You were innocent; you were *the victim of wrongdoing.* Flush out that wound-complicating sense of guilt.

On the other hand, *it may be genuine* rather than false guilt that lies like a dirt clod in the wound. Hateful thoughts and reactions against those who hurt you are sources of real guilt. Worse, it is not uncommon for a girl from a loveless home to seek "love" in the attention and arms of men. Memories of immoral behavior may even be worsened by remembered abortion. Obviously guilt for such real wrongs must be purged by wholehearted repentance. Whatever and however numerous your sins which complicate the original wrong, claim the promise,

If we confess our sins, he is faithful and just to forgive us our sins, and to cleanse us from all unrighteousness.
I John 1:9

The putrefaction of anger. Festering anger is the third kind of debris to be removed from the wound. It is tough to get rid of, because it has defiled the torn edges of the heart. In fact, you may even deny its presence; after all, as a Christian *you're not supposed to harbor anger.* Knowing this, you have pretended it was not there, denied its presence even to yourself. It has been hidden by the same feathers with which you covered the wound itself. But *look at it,* my friend: it is making a wretched, pussy mess. God speaks very plainly to us about the error of carnal anger.

> *The wrath of man worketh not the right-*
> *eousness of God.*
> *James 1:20*

Until you get rid of your anger, further progress toward healing is impossible. For anger hurts the Holy Spirit and hinders His working.

> *And grieve not the holy Spirit of God,*
> *whereby ye are sealed unto the day of re-*
> *demption. Let all bitterness, and wrath,*
> *and anger, and clamour, and evil speaking,*
> *be put away from you, with all malice.*
> *Ephesians 4:30-31*

Notice how God includes *all the forms* of anger in that passage: the explosive types, as in wrath; the restrained anger of hostility; and the bottled-up, redirected type known as malice. Whatever the specific type of your anger, it *blocks healing.*

Also, note the verb usage: "put away." That demands recognition and action. In other words, it is a matter, again, of our choosing—of our will. Anger over a hurtful childhood will not dissolve; it must be *cut away* with the scalpel of prayerful determination.

Anger, wrath, and malice make us want to lash back at or get even with those who hurt us. But God points us away from that negative human response:

> *Say not thou, I will recompense evil; but*
> *wait on the Lord, and he shall save thee.*
>> Proverbs 20:22

> *To me belongeth vengeance, and recom-*
> *pense; their foot shall slide in due time: for*
> *the day of their calamity is at hand, and*
> *the things that shall come upon them make*
> *haste.*
>> Deuteronomy 32:35

It is somehow satisfying to hold on to anger, isn't it?—to keep an emotional clenched fist, as it were. But, dear hurting woman, a clenched fist *cannot accept and hold the Physician's healing prescription.* All pain-worsening, scar-inflaming resentment must be cut away from your wounded self and be left with your wounded Savior.

Prescription Capsule #3—apply ointment. Please note the location of this point in the steps toward healing: it is the third in five—the *central* point. A wound inflicted by a child's home can never heal unless the ointment of *forgiveness* is applied to it.

The most common response coming from a home-wounded soul is "But I can't forgive—it's impossible!" Forgiving the heinousness of a crushing childhood home is, indeed, in the human sense, "impossible." The impossibility derives from our confusing obedience with emotion and supernatural ability with natural. Think briefly about these two levels.

Obedience versus emotion. Forgiveness is indeed impossible if we hold to the position that forgiveness cannot be real unless we *feel* forgiving. It immediately becomes possible if we forsake complicated feelings and fasten upon simple obedience to God's command.

Supernatural versus natural ability. Forgiveness is likewise impossible if its performance depends upon human capability: some demands are simply too big to be met with mortal strength. But when *God's* strength enters the picture, "impossibility" vanishes. We who balk at the difficulty of forgiveness need the lifted gaze of Jeremiah, when he said,

> *Ah Lord God! behold, thou hast made the*
> *heaven and the earth by thy great power*
> *and stretched out arm, and there is nothing*
> *too hard for thee.*
> *Jeremiah 32:17*

Just ten verses later, that all-powerful God Himself underscores His limitless capabilities:

> *Behold, I am the Lord, the God of all flesh:*
> *is there any thing too hard for me?*
> *Jeremiah 32:27*

So, then, will you refuse to forgive because of emotion? Or will you instead agree to forgive as an act of obedience? Will forgiveness be denied because of human limitation or allowed to be provided by God's unlimited ability? The stubborn, faithless "Impossible!" reaction not only keeps the lid on the ointment jar but also twists it more tightly closed.

It must be clear by this point that what is needed is, again, to leave and lean. Leave your own inability to forgive those of your home who hurt you and lean on that

One who delights to do the impossible. Listen as He speaks to those who, like you, are in distress:

> *And though the Lord give you the bread of*
> *adversity, and the water of affliction, yet*
> *shall not thy teachers be removed into a cor-*
> *ner any more, but thine eyes shall see thy*
> *teachers: and thine ears shall hear a word*
> *behind thee, saying, This is the way, walk*
> *ye in it, when ye turn to the right hand,*
> *and when ye turn to the left.*
>
> *Isaiah 30:20-21*

Listen to the very first pronouncement from that directive voice of the Teacher as it sounds a warning from Matthew 6:15:

> *But if ye forgive not men their trespasses,*
> *neither will your Father forgive your tres-*
> *passes.*

Note that there are no qualifications, no exemptions. Whoever those "men" are, whatever their relationship to you, however grievously they have misused you, *you must forgive*. To underline the all-encompassing character of the warning, heed Christ's words:

> *But I say unto you which hear, Love your*
> *enemies, do good to them which hate you.*
> *Bless them that curse you, and pray for*
> *them which despitefully use you.*
>
> *Luke 6:27-28*

We who bear scars from home wounding have been hurt by enemies within supposedly protective walls. We have been "despitefully used"—most traitorously. Still, *we are to forgive*.

Just a few verses later we hear Jesus emphasize the subject further.

But love ye your enemies, and do good, and lend, hoping for nothing again; and your reward shall be great, and ye shall be the children of the Highest: for he is kind unto the unthankful and to the evil. Be ye therefore merciful, as your Father also is merciful.

Luke 6:35-36

Not only will there be eternal reward for your having forgiven your home-side enemies; there will also be immediate benefit: the loosening of your own bonds. Unforgiveness harms its harborer more than it hurts its object. Lack of forgiveness actually makes its possessor captive to the offender. Ultimately, however, as the passage points out, we must forgive, we must be merciful, *because we are to reflect our heavenly Father's forgiving heart.* How can you or I fail or refuse to forgive when we remember the Lord Jesus as He, God in human flesh, hung dying on Calvary's cross. He looked down upon that surging, hatred-spewing mob to say, "Father, *forgive them,* for they know not what they do."

Are you overwhelmed by the immensity of forgiving that one or those ones who battered your being? God knows the struggle, my friend. Sense the intimacy of His understanding, the accuracy of your feelings, expressed in the following words from Isaiah 38:14.

Like a crane or a swallow, so did I chatter: I did mourn as a dove: mine eyes fail with looking upward: O Lord, I am oppressed; undertake for me.

71

And undertake He will! As you decide to obey by extending forgiveness, you yield to His will and working.

> *For it is God which worketh in you both to will and to do of his good pleasure.*
>
> *Philippians 2:13*

Immediately He loosens the cap on the ointment and the lovely aroma of *His ability,* replacing *your impossibility,* reaches your spirit.

> *Not that we are sufficient of ourselves to think any thing as of ourselves; but our sufficiency is of God.*
>
> *II Corinthians 3:5*

There is another possible area of obligation in cases where home offenses have come from those who are Christians: you may need to ask *their* forgiveness for any resentment, anger, or bitterness you have shown toward them. The principle was stated by the Lord Jesus.

> *If thou bring thy gift to the altar, and there rememberest that thy brother hath ought against thee; leave there thy gift before the altar, and go thy way; first be reconciled to thy brother, and then come and offer thy gift.*
>
> *Matthew 5:23-24*

Numberless Christians today, as well as their churches, are experiencing dwarfed spiritual lives because they have not handled offenses correctly.

Relational Realities

While forgiveness must be extended to our hurters, it may not mean easy or happy relationships with them. Distancing may need to be maintained. For instance, the father who sexually abused his daughters should not be allowed open-door acceptance: it would give him opportunity to repeat his offense against his grandchildren. The mother who continues to carp and criticize her daughter abusively should not be allowed to come for a three-month live-in visit. Very individualistic boundaries must be drawn in re-establishing relationships: what works in one situation might be unthinkable in another. Diligent consideration and earnest prayer should go into the decisions regarding ongoing relationships. I believe the Bible gives us insight into the dangers inherent in unwise relational proximity. Though referring primarily to adultery, the principle is clear.

> *Can a man take fire in his bosom, and his*
> *clothes not be burned? Can one go upon*
> *hot coals, and his feet not be burned?*
> Proverbs 6:27

When there continue to be "coals" and "fire" in the attitude, personality, or actions of the hurters, "taking them to the bosom" will be disastrous.

Final Forgiveness

Where sinfulness of self has built upon the sinfulness of others, as in the case of the wounded one's promiscuity, there also must be *forgiveness of self* after the sin has been repented of. Your own sin, whatever it has been, once truly repented of, *has been forgiven by God*. It must not remain unforgiven by you. Consider the following assurances of the Lord's *total* forgiveness.

> *I, even I, am he that blotteth out thy trans-*
> *gressions for mine own sake, and will not*
> *remember thy sins.*
> Isaiah 43:25

> *Behold, for peace I had great bitterness: but*
> *thou hast in love to my soul delivered it*

from the pit of corruption: for thou hast
cast all my sins behind thy back.

Isaiah 38:17

He will turn again, he will have compas-
sion upon us; he will subdue our iniquities;
and thou wilt cast all their sins into the
depths of the sea.

Micah 7:19

As far as the east is from the west, so far
hath he removed our transgressions from us.

Psalm 103:12

Prescription Capsule #4—set and splint broken bones.
Feathers are essential to a bird's ability to fly. But they are
not alone sufficient. Under the lightness of feather lies the
solidity of bone. That infrastructure is essential to a wing's
usefulness.

For a home-hurt person to soar into successful life and
service, the broken bones of *rejoicing* require mending. But
rejoice? After a lifetime of tears? Scripture tells us why
bone must be reknit.

The joy of the Lord is your strength.

Nehemiah 8:10

Without the supportive bone of rejoicing, we wounded
ones cannot struggle free from earth's binding. Review the
verses about God's cleansing from sin. The glorious fact of
our blood-washed soul should begin our heart's *rejoicing*.

Because thou hast been my help, therefore
in the shadow of thy wings will I rejoice.

Psalm 63:7

Resetting begins the process which will restore fractured rejoicing. Whereas bones have hung askew, rendering our wings useless, the rent edges now demand rejoining.

Realignment from gloom and negativism to rejoicing demands twin splints: *praise* and *gratitude.* Think about those two mending enablers.

Praise. Throughout the Bible, believers are urged to praise God. Praise is to be rendered to Him regardless of our circumstances. Rather than continuing to be *"under* the circumstances," we must determine to rise *above* them.

While a painful home background may be a *detriment,* it is not a *determiner.* Contemplate the contrast in the beautiful picture of promise given in Psalm 68:13.

> *Though ye have lien among the pots, yet*
> *shall ye be as the wings of a dove covered*
> *with silver, and her feathers with yellow gold.*

Further, praise is to be rendered without regard to emotion: it is not an "if I feel like it" matter; rather, we *simply obey* Scripture's command, letting Scripture itself be the empowerment.

Carefully consider four characteristics of the praise splint.

1. It is a means of fulfilling our "chief end," our ulti-mate purpose as ordained by God.

> *Whoso offereth praise glorifieth me: and to*
> *him that ordereth his conversation* [manner
> of life] *aright will I show the salvation of*
> *God.*
>
> *Psalm 50:23*

2. It is focused upon and exists for the benefit of God. True praise is not an emotional effusion or an act of personal gratification.

I will praise the Lord according to his right-
eousness: and will sing praise to the name
of the Lord most high.

Psalm 7:17

3. It is a means of unique fellowship with Christ and, by its sacrificial nature, reflects Christ.

Wherefore Jesus also, that he might sanc-
tify the people with his own blood, suffered
without the gate. Let us go forth therefore
unto him without the camp, bearing his re-
proach. For here have we no continuing
city, but we seek one to come. By him there-
fore let us offer the sacrifice of praise to
God continually, that is, the fruit of our
lips giving thanks to his name.

Hebrews 13:12-15

4. It is a means of spiritual beautification.

Rejoice in the Lord, O ye righteous: for
praise is comely for the upright.

Psalm 33:1

The second splint to support the newly aligned bone of rejoicing is *gratitude*. It, too, comes in obedience to Scripture, not in response to feelings.

In every thing give thanks: for this is the
will of God in Christ Jesus concerning you.

I Thessalonians 5:18

Oh that men would praise the Lord for his
goodness, and for his wonderful works to
the children of men! And let them sacrifice
the sacrifices of thanksgiving, and declare
his works with rejoicing.

Psalm 107:21-22

Generalized gratitude is not sufficient support for mending wings. Give thanks *for your hurt.* There *are* benefits even in the most painful experiences of life. Two examples may encourage you at this point.

Following a session in which I touched on childhood woundings, a young woman came to me in tears, protesting her inability to give thanks for her scarring from incest. Gently I led her to consider aspects of the matter which lay hidden in the haze of anger. The conversation went something like this:

"Didn't your father's treatment of you serve as a barrier against succumbing to teen-age sexual experimentation?"

She nodded slowly, mumbling, "Oh yes. I so hated what was happening at home that I never dreamed of going to bed with boys like some of the girls did."

"Didn't your knowledge, though premature, explicit, and repulsive, keep you from naive sexual involvement which otherwise might have trapped you?"

Again there was reluctant acknowledgment. "I knew all too well the signs of arousal in boys and men—and fled if they appeared."

"Wouldn't you be able to detect, almost instantly, attitudes and behavior in your daughters or your students which might indicate incest?"

Her response came quickly on that one: "Absolutely!" Then she paused as a smile gradually replaced her tears. "Yes. Yes, I see what you mean: there really are things to be specifically thankful for."

Her tears came again in a great rush as I posed the final question: "Are you not equipped—*because of* your suffering—to recognize and identify with pain in other people?" Because of her weeping, all she could do to signal the query's accuracy was nod vehemently.

That last-mentioned benefit from suffering—compassion—brings me to the second example. In this instance, it was a young missionary candidate with whom I was talking. Another incest victim, she confessed to enormous struggles, not only in her marriage relationship but also in the feeling that her background made her unfit for missionary service. Basically we went through the same question-and-answer procedure as detailed above. By the time our conversation drew to a close, her eyes were shining. I'll never forget her final, triumphant exclamation: "There's another *specific* thing to thank God for in my experience, Mrs. Jones. My husband and I are going to _____. Our mission board has told us that one of the major problems there is incest!" At that, we rejoiced together over God's ability to bring special ministry out of special mangling.

Now with the two parts of the splint in place, bind them firmly to the wing with the golden cord of Psalm 103.

Bless the Lord, O my soul: and all that is within me, bless his holy name. Bless the Lord, O my soul, and forget not all his benefits: who forgiveth all thine iniquities; who healeth all thy diseases; who redeemeth thy life from destruction; who crowneth thee with lovingkindness and tender mercies; who satisfieth thy mouth with good things; so that thy youth is renewed like the eagle's. The Lord executeth righteousness and judgment for all that are oppressed. He made known his ways unto Moses, his acts unto the children of Israel. The Lord is merciful and gracious, slow to anger, and plenteous in mercy.

*He will not always chide: neither will he
keep his anger for ever. He hath not dealt
with us after our sins; nor rewarded us according to our iniquities. For as the heaven
is high above the earth, so great is his
mercy toward them that fear him. As far as
the east is from the west, so far hath he removed our transgressions from us. Like as
a father pitieth his children, so the Lord pitieth them that fear him. For he knoweth
our frame; he remembereth that we are
dust. As for man, his days are as grass: as
a flower of the field, so he flourisheth. For
the wind passeth over it, and it is gone; and
the place thereof shall know it no more. But
the mercy of the Lord is from everlasting to everlasting upon them that fear him, and his
righteousness unto children's children; to such
as keep his covenant, and to those that remember his commandments to do them. The
Lord hath prepared his throne in the heavens;
and his kingdom ruleth over all. Bless the
Lord, ye his angels, that excel in strength,
that do his commandments, hearkening unto
the voice of his word. Bless ye the Lord, all ye
his hosts; ye ministers of his, that do his
pleasure. Bless the Lord, all his works in all
places of his dominion: bless the Lord, O
my soul.*

As you read through that magnificent psalm of praise
over and over again (or, even better, commit it to memory), your mind and heart will gradually but surely make
the praise personal. Each of us has cause to bless the Lord

for His marvelous Self and for His endless mercies which indeed are new every morning.

Our wings' broken bones are reset and splinted as we learn to say with the psalmist,

> *My heart is fixed, O God, my heart is fixed:*
> *I will sing and give praise.*
>
> Psalm 57:7

> *I will be glad and rejoice in thy mercy: for*
> *thou hast considered my trouble; thou hast*
> *known my soul in adversities.*
>
> Psalm 31:7

Prescription Capsule #5—Begin to use your wings. Wings are designed for *flight.* A bird confined to earth is pathetic and awkward. Yet what fear of flight must shake the flight-hungry bird whose wounded wings have kept her earthbound. How tentative must be that first launching. How frustrating must be her gradual resuming of flight.

We women with wounded wings should not expect immediate wholeness. Deep cuts demand time in order to heal. Broken bones mend slowly. Denuded flesh can only gradually be re-feathered. Let each trial movement of your wings be firmed by your *resting in the Person of Christ* and be energized by *renewing your mind with the Word of God.*

Resting in the Person of Christ

As in the earlier stages of healing, here too our loving Lord does what we cannot do. Frail humanity would keep us forever fearful, endlessly earthbound. But as the bird trusts its weight to the lifting air currents, so we must yield our fears to the enabling Creator. As we begin to exercise our wounded wings, we must commit ourselves fully to Jesus Christ. No matter how desperately we have been *failed* by those who should have loved, we can and will be *filled* by Him who ever loves.

> *When my father and my mother forsake*
> *me, then the Lord will take me up.*
> *Psalm 27:10*

> *As one whom his mother comforteth, so*
> *will I comfort you.*
> *Isaiah 66:13*

> *For in him dwelleth all the fullness of the*
> *Godhead bodily. And ye are complete in him.*
> *Colossians 2: 9-10*

> *How excellent is thy lovingkindness, O*
> *God! therefore the children of men put their*
> *trust under the shadow of thy wings.*
> *Psalm 36:7*

Let your weary, long-struggling soul experience the tender lift of Christ's comforting assurance of your completeness in Him. Herein lies the wonderful, the beautiful truth: genuine Christianity is much more than ritual and religious observances; it is a vital *relationship* with a living Person. That relationship is health-giving in every sense of the word. We are *literally* made complete *in Him* as the ever-living Balm of Gilead answers to every need of our home-hurt selves. Examine that blessed truth as it is evidenced in the names of Christ.

The hurtful past's ugliness fades in the radiance of the *Altogether Lovely One.*

Childhood's painful indelicacy is gentled by the *Lily of the Valley.*

The darkness of suffering gives way before the *Bright and Morning Star.*

Gray dreariness is forced aside by Him who is called *Wonderful.*

The questioning, distracted mind and heart grow calm in the *Counselor's* reassuring presence.

Conflict between puny self and overpowering evil vanishes before the face of the *Mighty God.*

Shattered, shivered existence becomes wholeness in the *Everlasting Arms* of the *Father.*

Turmoil, worry, and fear flee before the *Prince of Peace.*

The stench of sin dissipates in the glorious fragrance of the *Rose of Sharon.*

Plaguing confusion kneels quietly to the *Rabbi.*

Awful loneliness and isolation dissolve in the warmth of *Emmanuel,* God with Us.

Harsh treatment's abrasions lose their sting in the *Lamb of God's* soothing.

Lostness and aimlessness abate in the assured care of the *Great Shepherd.*

Months or years of groping along impenetrable walls turn to rejoicing in Him who is the *Door.*

And hunger of mind, heart, and soul are satisfied fully and permanently by the *Bread of Heaven.*

Oh, to *rest* in Christ! To realize that our richest opportunity to draw close to Him, to learn of Him, to experience His tender care, is in our extremity. At the end of ourselves, at the end of any mortal ability, there is the beginning of the Lord Jesus Christ's opportunity to undertake for us.

Renewing the Mind with God's Word

The Apostle Paul urges us,

> *And be* [constantly being] *renewed in the*
> *spirit of your mind.*
>
> *Ephesians 4:23*

As the living Word enables the soul's wings, so the written Word inspires the mind and heart. Unless we draw daily from the Bible, our flight to freedom will be sabotaged by fear and doubt. Passage after passage in the Bible urges our faint souls to take courage and encouragement. Tap into the strength of pertinent Scriptures as you prepare for and begin your flight.

First, each day's search of the Book might well begin with the confession and plea,

> *My soul melteth for heaviness: strengthen*
> *thou me according unto thy word.*
>
> *Psalm 119:28*

Second, we can be reminded of our joint venture with Christ as we seek courage moment by moment.

> *Wait on the Lord: be of good courage, and*
> *he shall strengthen thine heart: wait, I say,*
> *on the Lord.*
>
> *Psalm 27:14*

Third, we can launch upward into the clear skies of freedom with our hearts fixed on our heavenly Father's promise.

> *I will seek that which was lost, and bring*
> *again that which was driven away, and*
> *will bind up that which was broken, and*
> *will strengthen that which was sick.*
>
> *Ezekiel 34:16*

Finally, we need to recognize that our hurts probably have fostered negative thought patterns.

"I can't . . ."

"I'm not worthy of . . ."

"This thing is too big to shake free . . ."

Even worse than those generalized negative habits of thinking are mental replays from the past. Unbidden, they come into focus through memory's projector, intruding and unwanted, hated: sights, sounds, smells, emotional sensations, all of them robed in darkness. Such shadowed thinking should be banished as we walk with God, for

> *God is light, and in him is no darkness at all.*
> *I John 1:5*

Our heavenly Father does not keep the glorious light of His being to Himself. Rather, He says,

> *Light is sown for the righteous.*
> *Psalm 97:11*

One way we wounded ones can begin to banish darkness and benefit from the light is to consider God's thinking and let it switch on our own *lighted thinking.*

> *For my thoughts are not your thoughts, neither are your ways my ways, saith the Lord. For as the heavens are higher than the earth, so are my ways higher than your ways, and my thoughts than your thoughts.*
> *Isaiah 55:8-9*

> *For I know the thoughts that I think toward you, saith the Lord, thoughts of peace, and not of evil, to give you an expected end.*
> *Jeremiah 29:11*

Whether general or specific, *our mental negatives are wrong*. They are not just wrong in the sense of psychological debilitation: they are *sin*. They weigh us down, making us feel helpless and hopeless. The God who made the mind of man understands the importance of its focus. He says, for instance, of the human individual,

> *As he thinketh in his heart, so is he.*
> *Proverbs 23:7*

But God does not simply make the statement and leave it at that. In a Scripture passage mentioned earlier, God challenges the blood-washed believer to *control* that crucial mental capacity,

> *. . . bringing into captivity every thought to the obedience of Christ.*
> *II Corinthians 10:5*

Habits of thought, hurtful mental replays—all must become captive to our Spirit-enabled *will* and thus redirected. God puts what is needed into simplest form in order to ensure our comprehension.

> *Whatsoever things are true, whatsoever things are honest, whatsoever things are just, whatsoever things are pure, whatsoever things are lovely, whatsoever things are of good report . . . think on these things.*
> *Philippians 4:8*

Clearly, the uglies of the past disturb the mental focus God prescribes. For each old horror, we must choose a specific beauty upon which to think. Although there can be some benefit in choosing temporal beauties as a focus for thought, it is infinitely more beneficial to focus upon Him who is Himself the perfect pattern of all loveliness. In your Bible reading, concentrate upon the *character* of

God. That character is faceted with holiness, love, justice, mercy, and longsuffering. Recognize and rejoice in His perfect, eternal beauty.

To clinch the importance of renewing the mind with God's Word, we can look to I Timothy 4:15, in which God presents the keystone for the arch of successful Christian living:

> *Meditate upon these things; give thyself wholly to them; that thy profiting may appear to all.*

Observable spiritual profiting results from a right, spiritually controlled mindset. It produces not a wandering mind, a helpless mind, a tortured mind, but a *renewed* mind—a mind renewed by conscious, continuous intake and disciplined contemplation of *God's Word*.

CHAPTER SIX
THE FLIGHT ON WOUNDED WINGS

A bird—or a woman—with wounded wings: how can she rise confidently into the azure expanse of freedom from the past? How can she be assured of wholeness—of safe flight rather than of a plummet earthward? Only by personal commitment to and trust in Him who promises,

> *The eternal God is thy refuge, and underneath are the everlasting arms.*
> *Deuteronomy 33:27*

It will be important to remember that verse because there almost certainly will be variations of duration and height in our flying as we use our restored wings. However uneven our flight performance from day to day, however often we may lose heart and retreat earthward, however long the time needed to learn soaring, confident, unwavering flight, there *always* is the safety net of God's everlasting arms beneath us.

In this final chapter I want to direct your attention, wounded one, to God's Word, paralleling points made earlier. Only what He says is important. Tenderly, accurately, He speaks to our every need as wounded ones.

Look Up with a High Heart

Earth's dust and your wings' wounds have held you long enough. You are going to *mount above* the earth, my friend; you are going to *use the wings of your soul* as they were intended.

So, looking up, what do you see? A frightening, awesome expanse of blue? Perhaps. But more important, you see your Heavenly Father's smile of encouragement and reassurance. You let your heart exult,

> *Thy mercy, O Lord, is in the heavens; and*
> *thy faithfulness reacheth unto the clouds.*
> *Psalm 36:5*

Look Up with Proven Faith

Healing from the death-dealing sickness of sin comes only by the power of God through an individual's faith in the precious, cleansing shed blood of Jesus Christ. Be reminded of God's power already shown to you so wonderfully in bringing you from the Egypt of sin.

> *Ye have seen what I did unto the Egyptians,*
> *and how I bare you up on eagles' wings,*
> *and brought you unto myself.*
> *Exodus 19:4*

The reality you have already experienced in being freed from sin's *hold* calls you higher now, to freedom from sin's *hurt.*

Look Up with Assurance of God's Call

It is not just your weary, aching heart itself that wants to soar; your Creator God yearns to have you break free. He is at work right now, drawing your eyes to the sky, making you forgetful of your former wing dragging. God will be with you from start to finish,

> *. . . as an eagle stirreth up her nest, fluttereth over her young, spreadeth abroad her wings, taketh them, beareth them on her wings.*
>
> *Deuteronomy 32:11*

Commit Yourself, Fears and All, to Flight

You don't have to pretend to be strong. You needn't depend upon your own scraggly courage in order to take to the air successfully. As you move toward the launching point, as you step shakily onto the branch from which you will start your flight, do so honestly admitting your trepidations.

> *My heart is sore pained within me: and the terrors of death are fallen upon me. Fearfulness and trembling are come upon me, and horror hath overwhelmed me. And I said, Oh that I had wings like a dove!*
>
> *Psalm 55:4-6*

There is one especially pervasive fear which may grip the heart of someone who bears home hurts: the fear of repeating the experienced horror should she herself become a parent. Numerous studies have shown that those who have been hurt themselves very often become hurters in turn. Lovelessness, physical abuse, alcoholism, incest—all are provably repeated from one generation to the next. The Bible acknowledges and warns against that tendency.

> *The Lord is longsuffering, and of great*
> *mercy, forgiving iniquity and transgression,*
> *and by no means clearing the guilty, visiting*
> *the iniquity of the fathers upon the children*
> *unto the third and fourth generation.*
> *Numbers 14:18*

That repetition, however impressive and depressing, *is a part of evil's chain.*

Be assured, however, that this repetitive cycle is no more unbreakable than was the sin which bound us before salvation. God the Father and the Lord Jesus Christ delight to be daily in the chain-smashing business.

> *Remember ye not the former things, neither*
> *consider the things of old. Behold, I will do*
> *a new thing; now it shall spring forth; shall*
> *ye not know it? I will even make a way in*
> *the wilderness, and rivers in the desert.*
> *Isaiah 43:18-19*

Trust Your Heaviness to the Currents of Buoyant Air

Invisible but real currents of air sustain the bird aloft. Invisible but real, the currents of God's loving grace will rise beneath and give lift to your new-stretched wings.

The Apostle Paul, that giant of Christian testimony and ministry, honestly admitted encumbrances and weakness which, he felt, militated against his effective service. But rather than remove them, God urged the burdened apostle onward in ministry's flight.

> *For this thing I besought the Lord thrice,*
> *that it might depart from me. And he said*
> *unto me, My grace is sufficient for thee: for*
> *my strength is made perfect in weakness.*
> *Most gladly therefore will I rather glory in*

*my infirmities, that the power of Christ
may rest upon me.*

II Corinthians 12:8-9

The same rising currents of grace will counteract the downward pull of our defeating memories and fears.

Counteracting *regret* is the assurance of joy.

*Weeping may endure for a night, but joy
cometh in the morning.*

Psalm 30:5

Lifting above *frustration* is the promise of freedom.

*Blessed are ye that weep now, for ye shall
laugh.*

Luke 6:21

Driving away the *sense of being cheated* is the wealth and warmth of a sustained personal relationship with God.

*Keep me as the apple of the eye, hide me
under the shadow of thy wings.*

Psalm 17:8

The gnawing of emotional starvation is quieted by abundant love from the great heart of God.

*How excellent is thy lovingkindness, O
God! therefore the children of men put their
trust under the shadow of thy wings.*

Psalm 36:7

The hurt of *damaged self-concept* is balmed by the soothing and enabling presence of Him who is all in all.

*He shall cover thee with his feathers, and
under his wings shalt thou trust: his truth
shall be thy shield and buckler.*

Psalm 91:4

The threat of *bitterness and anger* is dissipated by the displacement of vengefulness by surrender.

*Say not, I will do so to him as he hath
done to me: I will render to the man according to his work.*

Proverbs 24:29

*The Lord executeth righteousness and judg-
ment for all that are oppressed.*

Psalm 103:6

Now, once-wounded one, you are aloft in the blue sky of freedom. You are beginning to use your restored wings in the way they were intended. Still, there is more than *soaring* for the healed bird; there is also *singing*.

There will be times of storm and darkness ahead—times when fear is renewed and scars throb. At these times also, God speaks to His beloved bird. When wind and rain and darkness challenge, respond with assurance that the crippling is past; healing has come. Remember your cry for healing; recall God's positive response.

*O Lord my God, I cried unto thee, and thou
hast healed me.*

Psalm 30:2

*He healeth the broken in heart, and bin-
deth up their wounds.*

Psalm 147:3

Do not fear the momentary turbulence. No matter how fierce the winds, you are safe because you are protected by *His* wings.

I will trust in the covert of thy wings.
Psalm 61:4

In the deepest darkness a song can rise to your lips from the One "who giveth songs in the night" (Job 35:10).

Because thou hast been my help, therefore
in the shadow of thy wings will I rejoice.
Psalm 63:7

Who among us has not marveled at a bird's cheerful song even in storm? So too you and I, healed and borne aloft by our loving Lord, can sing against the beating tempests.

Make us glad according to the days wherein
thou hast afflicted us, and the years
wherein we have seen evil.
Psalm 90:15

Our song is of safety, of wellness, of praise. God has renewed not only our flight but also our nest where we may nurture healthy offspring.

Yea, the sparrow hath found an house, and
the swallow a nest for herself, where she
may lay her young, even thine altars, O
Lord of hosts, my King, and my God.
Psalm 84:3

Our song has a lovely, lilting melody even in storm. Its heavenly lyrics tell of our freedom from all that went before. God has given us "beauty for ashes, the oil of joy for mourning, the garment of praise for the spirit of heaviness" (Isa. 61:3).

> *Our soul is escaped as a bird out of the*
> *snare of the fowlers: the snare is broken,*
> *and we are escaped.*
>
> *Psalm 124:7*

Wholeness, however, is not an end in itself, wonderful as it is. God's dealing with us does not stop with healing: He wants us to use our triumph over hurt and our song of freedom to help others.

Paradoxically, our usefulness is tied to the fact that our scars, though healed, will not disappear. Indeed, they will ever remain tender. This should not discourage us, however. The tenderness is not a detriment; it equips us with special understandings and promptings that can enhance spiritual growth and ministry. How may this be?

First, we who have suffered from agonies imposed upon us by others can more deeply appreciate the immeasurable pain of body, mind, and soul that our Lord Jesus Christ *took upon Himself.*

Second, our scars can drive us to a closer companionship with Jesus Christ as our experience of His reality in healing makes us yearn to be ever near Him.

Third, our scars' tenderness can increase our consciousness of Heaven. Scriptures which may hold only vague interest for the unwounded are full to overflowing for us.

> *And God shall wipe away all tears from*
> *their eyes; and there shall be no more*
> *death, neither sorrow, nor crying, neither*
> *shall there be any more pain: for the former*
> *things are passed away.*
>
> *Revelation 21:4*

Finally, the lingering tenderness can yield compassion for others who hurt and special sensitivity in comforting them. The purpose and process are made clear by the One

> *. . . who comforteth us in all our tribulation,*
> *that we may be able to comfort them which*
> *are in any trouble, by the comfort wherewith*
> *we ourselves are comforted of God.*
>
> II Corinthians 1:4

Recently I began thinking deeply about the story Jesus told of the Good Samaritan. Why did that man, alone of the three traveling the road, feel compassion and extend practical care to the thieves' victim? Could it be that part of his motivation came from *his personal experience with suffering?* As a citizen of Samaria he was despised, considered a "dog" by neighboring Jews.

Whoever we are, wherever we are, the darkness of the past—our wounds, the dreariness of our souls' wings dragging in the dust for months or years—together with the brightness of the present—the blessed, gentle ministrations of the Great Physician, the terror and exhilaration of renewed flight—all fit us in a special way to draw close to those around us who are hurt and crippled.

Then, with a tact that comes only from common experience in suffering, we can point them to that One who alone has healing for their wounded wings in His own wings. We can stand beside them through the renewed hurt of treatment. We can steady for them the little branch we ourselves have used. We can pray for them as they, too, launch out into the glorious skies of victory.

Ultimately, then, my wounded friend, every scar from your yesterday, as you allow it to be touched by the hand of God, can become a *beauty mark* for today, tomorrow, and indeed for all eternity. I pray that it may be so.